19-10831 (4/01/67)

THE WALTER LYNWOOD FLEMING LECTURES
IN SOUTHERN HISTORY

Louisiana State University

OTHER PUBLISHED LECTURES IN THIS SERIES

The Repressible Conflict, 1830-1861
by Avery O. Craven

Three Virginia Frontiers
by Thomas Perkins Abernethy

South America and Hemisphere Defense
by J. Fred Rippy

The Plain People of the Confederacy
by Bell Irvin Wiley

Behind the Lines in the Southern Confederacy
by Charles W. Ramsdell

Lincoln and the South
by J. G. Randall

The Rural Press and the New South
by Thomas D. Clark

Plain Folk of the Old South
by Frank Lawrence Owsley

Confederate Leaders in the New South
by William B. Hesseltine

The Texas Revolution
by William C. Binkley

Myths and Realities
by Carl Bridenbaugh

The South Lives in History
by Wendell Holmes Stephenson

Civil War in the Making, 1815-1860
by Avery O. Craven

The Fall of Richmond
by Rembert W. Patrick

JOHN RICHARD ALDEN

The First South

LOUISIANA STATE UNIVERSITY PRESS
BATON ROUGE

Preface

The author is glad to express his thanks to the Louisiana State University for inviting him to offer The Walter Lynwood Fleming Lectures in Southern History. They are published here substantially in the form they were given.

He wishes to acknowledge also the helpful services of his research assistant, Mr. Richard Goff, graduate student in history at Duke University, and of Mrs. Mary Stevens, secretary of the Department of History of Duke University. He desires to express his gratitude to Professor Hugh Rankin for thoughtful suggestions.

JOHN RICHARD ALDEN

Duke University

v

Contents

Contents

THE FIRST SOUTH

(1)

The First South

We Americans who are not too familiar with our history harbor a haunting memory of an Old South—an Old South of broad plantations; of their gracious masters and charming mistresses; of humble, cheerful, and loyal slaves who rose occasionally in ferocious revolt; of poor whites fearing naught but the wrath of Heaven; of cotton, magnolias, and Spanish moss—an Old South menaced and at last overwhelmed and demolished by Northern masses and machinery. We see through a glass doubtfully, and it is surely true that every general idea we have of that Old South is subject to exception and fuller description. The thousands of earnest historians who have delved into its remains must and do tell us that it was not as we are accustomed to think it was. Herein it is not intended to try to correct and clarify your vision, erroneous as it may be, of that familiar Old South, but to limn as truthfully as talents and energies will permit an even older South, which shall be named for convenience the First South.

This First South existed during the years 1775–1789. It appeared with the American nation; it was christened as early as 1778; and it clashed ever more sharply with a First North during and immediately after the War of Independence. This First South did not hasten under the Federal Roof with swift and certain steps, but haltingly and uncertainly. Many of her people feared that the Federal cover would offer greater protection north of the Susquehanna than it would south of that river. It should not be said that their alarm was without cause, that they saw troubles which the future did not bring. They feared lest they become a minority in an American union dominated by a Northern majority, lest they suffer in consequence. Whatever may be the merits of measures since imposed upon the South by the North—and the West—it will not be denied that the South has felt the power of external American forces, especially since the middle of the nineteenth century.

Now this First South, the Revolutionary South, the South of Patrick Henry, Light-Horse Harry Lee, and John Rutledge, was not the Old South of John C. Calhoun nor that of Jefferson Davis. In essence, nevertheless, they were the same, for they were alike in land, climate, people, economy, and social order. Even with respect to political structure and relations with the North, they were not so different as historians have commonly conceived. The Old South sought to leave the Union and to form a new nation; the First South—and for similar reasons—was not at all sure in the years 1787–1789 that it was wise to become part of that Union. Indeed, surprising as it may be, there were those in South Carolina, especially William Henry Drayton, who feared that South Carolina might suffer from the tyranny of Congress by giving consent to the Articles of Confederation. To be sure, the doubts of the First South were set aside, and it ultimately endorsed the Constitution of 1787, while the doubts of the Old South regarding the Union became so great that it denounced and sought to leave the Union. Here we have, however, an important difference in degree, not opposites absolutely.

There may be captious scholars—are not scholars by definition captious?—who will go so far as to deny that there was a South in the Revolutionary time.[1] One may be tempted to find importance in

[1] The writer indicated briefly in his *The South in the Revolution, 1763–1789* (Baton Rouge, 1957) that there was such a South. So far as he is aware, none of the reviewers of that volume expressed dissent.

the fact that the First South and the Old South were geographically not the same. Obviously enough, the First South was definitely limited by the Mississippi, while the Old South stretched westward into the empire of Texas; the First South was principally on the Atlantic seaboard, while the Old South contained both that seaboard and the lower half of the valley of the Mississippi. No matter, for the limits of a section, unless they be remarkably narrow, do not determine whether or not it exists.

More seriously, it may be asserted that the First South cannot have been because it lacked unity. It has been well said by Carl Bridenbaugh that there were actually three or four societies in the states from Maryland to Georgia at the beginning of the Revolution: an aristocratic order on the shores of the Chesapeake; another in the Carolina Low Country; a frontier society in the Old West; and possibly a fourth society not easily described in central North Carolina. But if there were three, or even four, societies below the Mason-Dixon line, it must be remembered that these were not three or four permanent societies completely distinct from each other. Those of the Chesapeake and the Low Country actually had much in common, including well-established American aristocracies and very large bodies of Negro slaves; and that of the Old West was actually only a passing phenomenon, since it would vanish with the frontier. Nor did central North Carolina possess one which could easily and positively be distinguished from those of the Chesapeake and the Low Country. The social differences to be discerned in the First South were hardly more impressive than were those in the Old South, the existence of which is not frequently or forcefully denied. The First South was not monolithic; neither was the Old South. Again, during the period 1775–1789, as afterward, heat, geography, racial and national composition, economic pursuits, social order, and even political structure, were ties of unity rather than sources of discord below the Susquehanna. That such was so is proven by events, for the First South frequently behaved as a section before 1789. It may be added that it was increasingly taken for granted by political men of the Revolutionary generation that the South was a distinct area with special and common interests that could not be ignored in the affairs of the nation.

All of which is not to say that there was such a region generally or even frequently referred to in 1775 or 1789 as the South. That name was used on a few interesting occasions, but the region was usually described between those years as the "Southern states." It follows, then, that there was a South even before the name came into common use, a fact which hardly surprises, since the infant should precede the christening. Before the War of Independence the colonies were often divided by observers into "Eastern" and "Southern," the term "Eastern" covering New England, the word "Southern" including all the colonies from New York to Georgia. Sometimes "Northern" was used as a synonym for "Eastern." Thus in 1767, when advising General Thomas Gage to establish a military base at or near Manhattan, General Guy Carleton pointed out that such a fortified place would not only provide security for military stores but would also "separate the Northern from the Southern colonies." The division between "Eastern" and "Southern" endured through the early years of the war, a usage which has confused some historians, who have occasionally and forgivably assumed that no one could think of Pennsylvania or New Jersey as Southern. It is nevertheless true that a quarrel between men of the Delaware valley and New England troops in 1776 was referred to as one between Southerners and Easterners. Even at that time, however, the word Southern was acquiring a more restrictive meaning, the phrase "Middle states" being used more and more to describe New York, New Jersey, Pennsylvania, and Delaware. These "Middle states" with the "Eastern states" were increasingly put together as the "Northern states," another usage which long endured.

Quickly shorn of the Middle states, the Southern states became a South and a section. The limits of that section were, of course, only gradually established in the minds of men; indeed, they cannot now be firmly laid down between it and the Middle states. There was disagreement about its northern boundaries at the time, although no one doubted that the Carolinas and Georgia were part of it.

Strange to say, none other than George Washington, until the adoption of the Constitution, was reluctant to include Virginia within the First South. In 1787 and again in 1788 he refers in his correspondence to the Carolinas and Georgia as the "Southern states." In 1786 he invited Don Diego de Gardoqui, the official emissary of Spain to the United States, to pay a visit to Mount Vernon "if you should ever feel an inclination to make an excursion into the middle states." It is apparent that Washington, a stout nationalist even before the close of the War of Independence, wished to minimize the South and its special interests. But he was forced to recognize that they existed, and he too began to refer to the region between Pennsylvania and the Floridas as the "Southern states." Not until his first term as president did he fully realize the vitality of a Southern section that inluded Virginia. Becoming genuinely and even gravely alarmed, he urged his countrymen, in his Farewell Address, to soften their sectional antagonisms.

Except for Washington, I have found no Revolutionary worthy who would have drawn a line between Virginia and the South. And I have discovered only one other Founding Father who did not include Maryland in the "Southern states." That person was William Henry Drayton of South Carolina, who declared most emphatically in the winter of 1777–1778 that Virginia, the Carolinas, and Georgia formed "the body of the southern interest." Almost invariably, men in public life perplexed by North-South contests said or assumed that Maryland belonged to the Southern connection. Frequently politicians referred to difficulties between the eight Northern states and the five Southern ones. Others indicated that the North and the South were set apart by the Susquehanna River.

The prevailing view was put flatly in 1787 by Charles Pinckney of South Carolina, who declared, "When I say Southern, I mean Maryland, and the states to the southward of her."

However Maryland may be classified—Southern, border, or Northern—in the nineteenth and twentieth centuries, it is appropriate to place her with the South in the Revolutionary time. It is true that central Maryland and western Maryland, even then, were countries of farms rather than plantations; of corn, wheat, and livestock instead of tobacco; of yeoman farmers rather than white masters and black slaves. But it should be remembered that only eastern Maryland, a plantation region, was then fully settled. It is also true that Maryland was slightly more commercial and a trifle more urban than Virginia. Nevertheless, in the days of the Revolution, the two states above and below the Potomac were fundamentally identical both economically and socially. Maryland at that time belonged with Virginia, and both with the South.

It was assumed soon after the close of the War of Independence that the northern limits of the South were on the Ohio as well as the Mason-Dixon line. Before the end of that conflict Virginia abandoned her claim to the Old Northwest; and Southerners generally sanctioned the Northwest Ordinance, which effectively placed the region between the Ohio, the Mississippi, and the Great Lakes outside the South. There was, however, agreement among politicians Northern and Southern, that the new settlements of Kentucky and Tennessee were Southern. As parts of Virginia and North Carolina until after the adoption of the Constitution, it could hardly be doubted at the time that they were parts of the South. Nor should we doubt it, even though we may not share the alarm then felt by leaders of New England because they saw the occupation of Kentucky and Tennessee as evidence that the South was expanding at the cost of the North. The Revolutionary South included the settlements of Boonesborough and Nashville as well as Annapolis and Savannah.

Proportionally to the remainder of the Union, the Revolutionary South was the largest South, both in size and in people. In fact, the Southern population in the first Federal census of 1790 was only a trifle smaller than that of the rest of the nation, there being then counted about 1,900,000 persons below the Mason-Dixon line, slightly more than 2,000,000 above it. At that time Virginia was by far the most populous state, and North Carolina ranked fourth, behind Massachusetts and Pennsylvania. Had not Maine been a part of Massachusetts, North Carolina would have been the third state in numbers. Moreover, there were Southerners who believed that population was increasing more rapidly in the South than elsewhere. These facts had influence upon the decision of the Southern states to ratify the Constitution, for it could be asserted with some show of reason that the South would soon surpass the remainder of the Union in numbers. It was not fully realized, perhaps, that the three-fifths provision of the Constitution respecting the slaves would place the South in a minority position in the national House of Representatives, even in the composition of the first Congress based on the census. Besides, as it turned out, the appearance of more rapid growth in the Southern population was illusory—the gap between North and South soon widened rather than diminished, as the census of 1800 indicated.

Hitherto it has been asserted rather than shown that there was a Revolutionary South. Nor will all the proof that such was the case be marshalled in detail at this point. Much of the best sort of proof, consisting of sectional quarrels, will be offered later. Nevertheless, it may be well to bring forth at this point certain fundamental reasons why the First South was crudely a unit with interests and views opposed to those of the rest of the Union.

Nature herself certainly set apart the South, giving to the South tropical summers, long growing seasons, and mild winters. Nature also gave soils and waters suitable for growing vast quantities of tobacco and rice, products which could be consumed only in small part in the South, which were much desired by foreign peoples, especially Europeans. In the Chesapeake region tobacco growing long seemed to be the best road to wealth, although it obviously was a road marred by ruts and mudholes; in the Carolina Low Country after the middle of the eighteenth century rice growing, together with the production of indigo, offered a surer and smoother highway to affluence. In consequence, the South had become before the Revolution a country of general farming and also of highly specialized farming that sent forth exports in great quantity and value. Meanwhile, the people of the Northern colony-states, with their colder climates, continued to engage in general farming, fishing, and lumbering, but turned increasingly toward internal trade, shipbuilding, sea-borne commerce, and manufacturing. Thus the economic pursuits of

South and North became not only different, but often seemingly opposed. Instances enough of clashes over economic issues in the Revolutionary time will be offered later.

The special farming of the South was also the chief cause for a profound racial divergence between the sections, since the raising of tobacco and rice led to the importation into the South of large numbers of Negroes. In the Northern states, except for Delaware, at the time of the Revolution, the Negroes formed only small minorities. Below the Mason-Dixon line it was otherwise, for in the South 35 of every 100 persons were Negroes. They made up a full 30 per cent of the populations of Maryland and North Carolina, 40 per cent of that of Virginia, and more than half of that of South Carolina. The Negroes, burgeoning in numbers because of the special farming of the South, in turn helped to perpetuate such farming. The Southerners could think of few occupations for them beyond toil in tobacco rows, care of rice plants, weeding of corn, and other field tasks. Moreover, the presence of the Negro, together with the Southern economy and climate, tended to discourage white immigration, a fact which was noted by and which alarmed some astute Southern observers even be-

fore 1775, a fact which census returns afterward
made evident to all who would bother to read
such reports.

Economic and racial divergences between South
and North brought with them serious social varia-
tion. Negro slavery was quite fixed upon the South,
while it had few and weak roots above the Susquehanna. Slavery and special farming widened
social cleavage among the Southern whites, giving
added strength to the principle of aristocracy
below the Mason-Dixon line. At the day of the
Revolution there were admittedly socially superior
persons in the Northern colony-states, chiefly
country magnates and wealthy merchants. They
were fewer and less powerful in New England than
they were in the Middle states; and they were more
conspicuous and more influential on the Chesapeake and in the Carolina Low Country than they
were on the Hudson or the Delaware. Even North
Carolina had its Tidewater aristocracy. The tobacco and rice lords often could not see eye-to-eye
with the dominant middle-class men of the North.
John Adams did not feel unmixed respect and liking for the "nabobs" of South Carolina whom he
met in Congress after 1774; nor did the aristo-
cratic-minded Southern delegates feel unadulter-

ated admiration for the Yankees with whom they considered men and measures in New York and Philadelphia.

There were indeed important differences between the Northerners and the Southern whites as a whole in the Revolutionary time, as Thomas Jefferson pointed out in a letter to the Marquis de Chastellux in 1785. He said:

In the North they are	In the South they are
cool	fiery
sober	voluptuary
laborious	indolent
independent	unsteady
jealous of their own liberties, and just to those of others	zealous for their own liberties, but trampling on those of others
interested	
chicaning	generous
superstitious and hypocritical in their religion	candid
	without attachment or pretentions to any religion but that of the heart

"These characteristics," asserted the thoughtful Virginian, became "weaker and weaker by gradation from North to South and South to North, insomuch that an observing traveller, without the aid of the quadrant may always know his latitude by the character of the people among whom he finds himself. It is in Pennsylvania that the two characters seem to meet and blend and to form a people free from the extremes both of vice and virtue." We need not accept precisely the opinion of Jefferson regarding either Northerners or Southerners, and we may also doubt that the Golden Mean existed in Pennsylvania, but there is obvious merit in his analysis. Assuredly, it is significant that he saw contrasts, even mistakenly, and that he thought them important enough to relate to his French friend.

Since colonial federation, though occasionally talked about and even planned, never was undertaken, serious clash between North and South did not appear before 1775. There were many contests between colony and colony, but none in which the one region was challenged by the other. It is true that jealousies of a sectional nature arose because some Southern colonists fancied that their Northern brethren were too hasty and too forward in asserting American rights against Britain during the decade before Lexington and Concord. Conversely, Northern defenders of American rights sometimes felt that the Southerners moved too slowly and too uncertainly. When the program of general nonimportation of British goods was rather hastily abandoned in the Northern ports after the repeal of most of the Townshend duties in 1770, just as nonimportation was being effectively put into force in South Carolina, there was genuine resentment in Charleston.[2] But here we have passing irritations rather than enduring troubles. Actually the struggles of the Americans against Britain before 1775, and the War of Independence especially, served to bring the Americans together by supplying them with a common, dangerous, and detested enemy.

Indeed, let us not forget that there were many and powerful forces pushing the Americans together in both the colonial and Revolutionary epochs. Too much may be made of economic and social antagonisms between North and South; too little heed may be given to unifying vigors. It should be recalled that almost all the Americans, save the Negroes, had a common background in the British Isles and that part of the European con-

[2] Yankee Josiah Quincy, Jr., found in Charleston in 1773, "a general doubt of the firmness and integrity of the Northern colonies."

tinent west of the Elbe River; that nearly all of them spoke English—English with perhaps fewer differences between North and South than afterward; and that they shared the benefits and evils of an English cultural and political heritage. Moreover, the Americans had felt alike the influence of similar elements in their New World environment. At the opening of the Revolutionary time they were aware of their oneness, a fact indicated by their ever-increasing use of the term American as descriptive of all the inhabitants of the Thirteen Colonies—a usage which also became dominant in Britain after 1763. The beginning of the Revolutionary contest with Britain near the end of the French and Indian War added, as has been suggested, a new dynamic toward unity, Britain the foe of America as a whole. Northerners and Southerners had a common political enemy before 1775; even more important, they were faced by a common military antagonist between 1775 and 1783; after the close of the War of Independence, they continued to share fears of British and European aggressions. Those who fear the same menaces, those who fight the same foes, tend to feel that they are one.

Above all, the War of Independence aroused an

American emotion. Virginians served at Boston and Quebec, Carolinians at Brandywine and Germantown, Yankees at Trenton and Yorktown. The "hard core" of the Revolutionary forces was the Continental army; and "Continental" was, or rather soon became, a synonym for "American." Few of the men who served in it could afterward be easily convinced that they fought only for their home state, or for a South, or for a North.[3] For the Continental veteran, officer and man, and doubtless almost to a man, America was his country. None were more devoted to the nation than were Virginia soldiers George Washington, Light-Horse Harry Lee, Daniel Morgan, and John Marshall. If one had suggested to a Southern veteran that he had not found Connecticut or New Jersey troops remarkably congenial, he would almost surely have responded that such was sometimes the case, but that they had been, when all was said and done, true and worthy comrades in a great cause.[4] And

[3] A Virginia newspaper reported in June, 1780 that "Captain Lieutenant Richard Coleman of Spotsylvania county, fell in the defence of his country on the 29th day of May . . . in South Carolina."

[4] In early acquaintance Southerners often disliked New Englanders, whose worst qualities were only too evident, whose finer ones required time to discover. Even in the long run the Yankees were more likely to inspire respect rather

that cause could hardly be the creation of a string of small independent countries along the Atlantic coast; or of two or three nations; or even of one confederacy so feeble at its heart that it would be absurd to describe it as an American union.

American nationalism during the Revolutionary era should not be considered minor, nor were the forces creating and supporting it meager or temporary. The same should be said for the divisive tendencies of sectionalism. In that era nationalism was to triumph.

The contest between South and North began even before the Declaration of Independence. In the first general American assembly—in the First Continental Congress in 1774—came the first quarrel. It was, as were most of such struggles before 1789, economic in nature. When that body considered measures to compel Parliament and Crown to change their course to American wishes, it decided to use a weapon which had become familiar, a boycott of British goods. There was no

---

than fondness in the Southerner. James Fallon of South Carolina offered an early impression of them in 1779: "The inhabitants hereabouts [Fishkill, N.Y.] are all Yankees. I mean not to reflect *nationally;* but their manners are, to me, abhorrent. I long to leave and get clear of their oddities. They are, for the most part, a *damned* generation."

sectional disagreement regarding the use of this boycott, even though the importation of Negro slaves was also forbidden. Nor was there any difficulty between North and South because the Congress decreed nonconsumption of British goods, this measure being calculated to prevent merchants from pulling profits out of scarcities. It was otherwise when the delegates decided to use the club of nonexportation to Britain and the British West Indies, in case of need, the date for cessation being set at September 10, 1775. The delegates from South Carolina, except for Christopher Gadsden, asked that rice and indigo be excepted from the embargo, and so raised a controversy.

In this clash varying economic interests were basic. On the surface, the South Carolina men in the Congress were asking a special favor for the Low Country; from their point of view they were merely requesting equal sacrifice from all sections. Because of British law and other circumstances rice and indigo markets in England and the British West Indies were very important to South Carolina. Were exportation of those products to those markets forbidden, the Low Country planters, almost utterly dependent upon sales of rice and dye stuffs, must suffer grievously. The Northern colonies would be able to sell outside Britain and the islands, as they had in the past; and even the Chesapeake colonies, their tobacco going largely to London, Bristol, and Liverpool because of Parliamentary law, could escape the worst effects of the self-inflicted punishment of embargo by turning to wheat-growing. Even so, the attitude of the South Carolina delegation was not generous, especially with respect to their fellow planters of the Chesapeake; and Gadsden was prepared to offer a total sacrifice. When Northerners in Congress cried favoritism, the dominant Carolinians withdrew their request for excepting indigo; and for the sake of creating a solid front against Britain, the free sending of South Carolina's rice to sea was permitted. Thus the quarrel was resolved by concession on the part of the others to the Low Country planters. It has been suggested that Gadsden's colleagues should not be judged too harshly; it is worthy of mention that the news of the arrangement did not create great joy in Charleston. Early in 1775 the South Carolina Provincial Congress, considering the situation, and perhaps feeling some pangs of conscience, defeated a motion to ban rice exportation by the narrow margin of 87 to 75.

Early in the Second Continental Congress another issue threatened sectional trouble, and was settled in such fashion that nationalism won a victory of vast consequences. When that body decided to form a Continental army, it was immediately faced by a momentous question: who should be its commander in chief? It is now well known that George Washington had many merits and that these were not entirely unfamiliar in Philadelphia. However, New Englanders were inclined to favor the appointment of a Yankee, Israel Putnam or some other hero of the lands east of the Hudson. Aware that unity would be secured by choosing a Southerner and that Washington was otherwise suitable, John and Samuel Adams consented to the appointment of the Virginia colonel. The decision did allay sectional feeling at the time.[5] Far more

[5] Long afterward, the Reverend Jonathan Boucher, whose acquaintance with Washington was hardly intimate, said the Southern colonists feared in 1775 that they would be dominated by a Northern army after independence had been achieved and that Washington's acceptance of the supreme command was dictated, "more than anything else," by a desire to prevent such a horrid outcome. At the time, Governor Jonathan Trumbull of Connecticut expressed a hope that the selection of Washington would "cement the union between the Northern & Southern colonies—& remove any jealousies of a N England army (if they should prove successfull) being formidable to the other provinces." In the summer of 1776 General Persifor Frazer of Pennsylvania also commented from

important, the personal fortunes of Washington became entwined with those of a national army. He felt the adverse effects of particularism and sectionalism in the war effort as could no other person. It may even be said that Washington's fame came to depend in part upon the creation of a permanent American union. Were his military achievements to lead to the making of a number of small American nations, he could hardly be the mighty figure he became. Whether the commander in chief was fully conscious that his glory was inextricably linked with that of the United States is a question of no importance. Such was the fact; and there was no more sturdy, no more steady nationalist in the South than the great Virginian at the end of the war. As he said farewell to his army, he begged that his comrades give their support to a solid union; and he was to be more responsible than any

---

Fort Ticonderoga upon fear of New England. "No man was ever more disappointed in his expectations respecting New Englanders than I have been. They are a set of low, dirty, griping, cowardly, lying rascals. There are some few exceptions and very few. . . . You may inform all your acquaintance not to be afraid that they will ever conquer the other provinces (which you know was much talked of), 10,000 Pennsylvanians would I think be sufficient for ten times that number out of their own country. All the Southern troops live in great harmony."

other man for putting the Constitution into force. We are all accustomed to praising the man of Mount Vernon for his military merits, and there have been those who have contended—I think, without full cause—that his services as president were even more remarkable than those he offered in his campaigns and battles. Let it not be forgotten that he was also the man above all others responsible for the general adoption of the Constitution. Many a great American of his time and later ones was to be first a nationalist and later a regionalist, or a sectionalist and then a nationalist—the names of John C. Calhoun and Daniel Webster come to mind. Not so with Washington, who stoutly and firmly fought against sectional prejudice in the Continental army, in the struggle over the Constitution, and in the presidency. Even now we perhaps do not value fully his devotion to the nation. First in war, first in peace, first in the hearts of his countrymen, he was also first in his allegiance and contribution to American unity.

Although the appointment of Washington as commander in chief was a triumph for nationalism, sectionalism also had its victories during that part of the Revolutionary War which preceded the Declaration of Independence. It will be recalled that the movement toward complete separation from Britain during the first fifteen months of the Revolutionary War was accompanied by a movement toward an American union. Thus when Richard Henry Lee of Virginia introduced in Congress on June 7, 1776, his famous resolution declaring that "These United Colonies are and of right ought to be free and independent states," he also called for the making of an American federation. By most public men in Congress and out, independence and political union were considered as virtually inseparable. Indeed, there were Patriot leaders in the spring of 1776, including Patrick Henry, who asserted that the Americans should marry each other before they declared themselves divorced from the British. These claimed that independence would be easier to achieve if union were secured before issuing a formal announcement that America had left the empire. As early as the fall of 1775 the Revolutionary legislature of North Carolina indicated its disapproval of the famous plan of confederation submitted by Benjamin Franklin because it gave New England larger representation in the federal legislature than the North Carolina men were willing to concede to it. This was much to the satisfaction of Josiah Martin, the last royal governor of North Carolina, who claimed that Franklin's arrangements would enable the North "to give law" to the South and who gleefully asserted that the North would use its power, since there was in New England a "lust of domination."

Any argument which might serve to sow dissension among the Patriots was welcomed by Josiah Martin, and also by James Anderson, another supporter of the Crown, who sought to frighten the South to the advantage of Britain. In a pamphlet published at Edinburgh in 1776 Anderson predicted that an independent American union would be disastrous for the Southerners. They would form a minority in an American legislature, and their economic interests would be injured to the benefit of those of the Northerners. Time would bring so great exasperation at the South that the Southerners would seek to form a new nation. They would not be permitted to leave the union peacefully; and, fewer in numbers and enervated by heat, they would be defeated in war. Thereafter they would live in a state of inferiority and subjection to the North. It turned out that there was basic truth coupled with error in Anderson's calculations and predictions. And his reputation as a prophet must also suffer because he foresaw what he wished to foresee, that parting from England would not bring such sweet tomorrows to the Americans.

Josiah Martin and James Anderson, not friends to American freedom, told the Southerners they should not join an American union. Other men not hostile to independence said such a union could not be formed because of the contrarieties which existed in the Thirteen. In the middle of the 1780's it was frequently suggested by Americans not seeking to return to the British empire that two or even three confederacies would rise along the Atlantic coast. One of these would be Southern, including Maryland and the states to her southward. There might be two confederations north of the Mason-Dixon line, one in New England and another composed of the Middle states; or New England and the Middle states might form one union. As late as 1788 Patrick Henry was accused, and not entirely without reason, of seeking to create a Southern confederacy. There were even Southern public men of the Revolutionary period who believed, because of the power of local loyalties, that the Thirteen States must go their separate ways. So Thomas Burke of North Carolina asserted in 1778 that an American union was a "chimerical project." So William Blount of the same state in July, 1787, declared, "I still think we shall ultimately and not many years . . . be separated and distinct governments perfectly independent of each other." To be sure, both Burke and Blount afterward changed their minds.

Because of the difficulty of assessing the conflicting forces which supported state loyalties, regional confederacies, and general union, no one could assuredly predict during the twelve years after the Declaration of Independence what political form or forms the Americans would adopt. It may be guessed that personalities, and even chance, affected the outcome, despite the conviction of George Bancroft that the course of events was personally and intimately directed by the Deity.

It could be safely predicted, however, that troubles must arise between South and North in a union with a central government possessing substantial powers. Sectional conflicts continued throughout the war. When Washington's army was undergoing its ordeal at Valley Forge in the winter of 1777–1778, Virginians and South Carolinians were voicing alarm lest Congress under the Articles of Confederation possess too great authority, to the detriment of Southern interests. That body during the years 1781–1787 was often riven by strife between South and North. Southern fears of Northern domination appeared in the Philadelphia Convention of 1787, and were frequently and forcefully asserted in the contests over ratification of the Constitution which took place below the Mason-Dixon line. Those fears were often based in part upon acute reasoning; indeed, in view of later occurrences, few will say they were without some solid foundation.

(2)

Sectional Struggles in the
Continental Congress

There is little glamour in the day-to-day proceedings of a legislative body, and glory is not
easily won in the committee room. Heroes of party
caucuses and partisan debate often receive less at-
tention than they deserve. On the other hand, the
achievements of men displayed on the battlefield,
in art, and in literature are comparatively discern-
ible and dramatic. Hence we tend to worship
George Washington, and to praise highly Tom
Paine. Hence most of us know little about the trials
and triumphs of the Congress during the Revolutionary period. Too much has been said about its
weaknesses and its failures. A few adulators of
Washington would have it that the chief purpose
of Congress during the War of Independence was
to serve as a stumbling block for the commander in
chief. Others have proclaimed that that body ac-
complished little in the years between the Peace of

Paris and the inauguration of Washington. Let it be said that the Congress did very well in trying circumstances, that it is difficult to see how it could have performed much better than it did. Yet it is true that the delegates often failed, and it is only too evident that they were given to bickering and serious contention. Distrust of New England was chronic among the Southern deputies throughout the years 1776–1787; and clashes between the Yankees and the plantation men in that body were frequent and warm. Indeed, these jealousies and quarrels turned South against North, and North against South. There were men from the South who refused to look upon their Northern colleagues as enemies, who sought to understand their point of view, who were willing to make reasonable compromises with them. Many of the Southern men, however, saw as did delegate Cyrus Griffin of Virginia, who said in 1778:

Congress exhibit not more than two or three members actuated by patriotism. Great questions are carried every day in favour of the East-ward, and to the prejudice of the Southern States. Great questions are now upon the carpet and if determined in the affirmative will do excessive damage to Virginia and Maryland particularly. At present we are under secrecy—perhaps in a little time I shall think myself obligated to quit Congress; I will not sit in a house whose proceedings I cannot assent to with honor, nor is it in my abilities to oppose them with success. . . . I am apprehensive that in getting free from oppression in one quarter, we are likely to establish it in another; by avoiding one set of plunderers we are certain to fall into the clutches of a still more dangerous set.

Nevertheless, despite fears, irritations, hot debates, and very real issues, none of these clashes, nor all of them put together, became ultimate.

One sectional dispute which continued in Congress during most of the war is of special interest because Negro slavery was enmeshed in it. It began as early as the fall of 1775, when Washington was struggling to put the army about Boston in order and discipline. In that army there were some Negroes fighting for the freedom of white men, if not their own. On September 26 Edward Rutledge, delegate from South Carolina, moved that those Negroes, whether slave or free, be discharged from service. Rutledge contended that they could not be expected to render service equally with whites because they had less at stake. There was doubtless a bit of truth in the argument, but it is evident enough that he disliked the placing of arms in the hands of the Negroes. Suppose that the dark-skinned men of the Carolina Low Country, far more numerous than the planters who owned them, were given weapons? That was a question which deeply disturbed Rutledge, at a time when some hundreds of Negroes, called forth by Lord Dunmore to serve for King and their own freedom, were rallying to the British standard in Virginia. The motion of the aristocratic planter was "strongly supported by many of the Southern delegates," but it was opposed with equal ardor by their Northern colleagues; and it was defeated, for John Adams and others could not agree with the gentlemen of the rice-indigo country that the Negro might become a grave menace. However, the men from the Far South did not debate without effect. In accordance with a recommendation from Washington, the Congress resolved in January, 1776, to restrict Negro enlistment in the future to those already in service.

But this resolution by no means put an end to the use of Negro troops in Northern regiments, nor did it permanently push aside thoughts of enlisting other Negroes, including slaves, in large numbers. Rather oddly, the idea of using Negro slaves was revived and pushed in Congress by South Carolinians. In the Revolutionary time, when there was no Northern campaign against slavery in the South, there was a minority in South Carolina that dared to assail the institution. Foremost among its enemies there were Henry and John Laurens, father and son, veteran politician and brave young Continental officer, two conspicuous adornments of the Low Country aristocracy. John Laurens urged as early as 1776 that slaves be offered personal freedom in return for military service in the cause of the rights of mankind. Three years later it seemed to him that there was a chance of securing the adoption of the scheme in his home state and Georgia. Immediately before the close of 1778 the British had captured Savannah, and it seemed likely that they would undertake the conquest of South Carolina—as they did in 1780. Although the Patriots of the two states in the Far South were spirited and devoted—as *they* were to prove in a dozen battles and a thousand skirmishes—they were too few to hold their own against George III's regulars, the numerous Tories of the Deep South, and hostile Indians on the frontier. In 1779 Governor John Rutledge of South Carolina sent General Isaac

Huger northward to beg help from Congress. Young Laurens urged his father, a member of that body, to use his influence toward securing its consent for enlisting slaves for the defense of the two states. He offered to serve with these slave troops. Without hope that the project could succeed, Henry Laurens nevertheless supported it. General Huger voiced his approval, and so did William Henry Drayton, who then formed with the older Laurens the South Carolina delegation in Congress.

Seeking the blessing of Washington upon the plan, the older Laurens told the commander in chief that three thousand Negro troops would not only assure the safety of the Far Southern states but would compel the British to retreat to St. Augustine in Florida and perhaps even to abandon that British stronghold. Washington foresaw difficulties. If the Patriots raised slave troops, the British might copy their example, and the British would be able to equip more Negroes than could the Americans. Moreover, he believed that slaves not permitted to fight in exchange for their freedom would become restless. But even without the solid endorsement of Washington, Henry Laurens and Drayton proceeded to ask Congress to purchase the release of three thousand slaves in the two

38

states, to arrange for placing them in military service, and to make plans for freeing the survivors at the close of the war.

During some weeks, this scheme, which must have dealt a heavy blow to slavery, seemed on the road to success. Since it was proposed by the South Carolina delegation and backed by General Huger, it was unanimously sanctioned by a Congress perplexed by many difficulties and eager to secure help wherever possible. However, the delegates knew that the project could not be executed without the consent of the two states so intimately concerned, and stipulated that no action be taken without their concurrence. Young Laurens hurried to Charleston and begged the legislature of South Carolina to endorse it. But its members, even though the outlook for the Patriots in the Far South was not brightening, gave him a cold reception. A few spoke up for the scheme, but a large majority vigorously opposed it, and it was rejected, "blown up with contemptuous huzzas."

So South Carolina struck down the plan advanced by the Laurenses. But it was not yet dead. After Yorktown, young Laurens, then in service in his native region, again urged the lawmakers of his state to take up the scheme. Heavy losses among the Patriots of South Carolina and Georgia were a powerful argument in its behalf. Militarily, they were almost exhausted; and the British still had thousands of troops in Charleston, Savannah, and St. Augustine. Moreover, General Nathanael Greene, commander of the Continental forces in the South which had performed brilliantly but were also scanty and weakened, gave powerful support to the scheme, urging the newly revived legislatures of the two states to adopt it. Now it received serious consideration from the South Carolinians. But it could be believed in view of the stunning Franco-American victory at Yorktown that the war was drawing to a close. There were many votes for the plan in the South Carolina assembly, but not a majority; nor was it approved in Georgia. And so a venture which must have supplied powerful force toward the eventual destruction of slavery in the end rather narrowly failed.

The most serious sectional controversy during the War of Independence, and one which continued after the bullets had ceased to whistle, arose, inevitably, when the Patriots undertook to make a national constitution. The provisions of such a basic document might have the most profound effects into the most distant future, consequences far greater than those which could proceed from Congressional resolutions. Because there was a widespread fear of central tyranny in the Northern states as well as the Southern ones, the first constitution of the United States, the Articles of Confederation, provided for a weak central government. Since neither section then wanted a powerful one, clash between them regarding its powers, methods of representation, and appointment of financial burdens was reduced. Nevertheless, the making of the Articles during the years 1776–1777 and attempts to revise them which continued for a decade created much sectional ill feeling within Congress and without. Peculiarly sharp were debates over distribution of the cost of the central regime. But other issues were raised and squabbled about; and in South Carolina the need for constitutional protection of Southern interests against Northern tyranny was raised in startling fashion.

When the men at Philadelphia began in 1776 to go into the business of constitution-making, Edward Rutledge was already distrustful of national power. Said Rutledge: "The idea of destroying all provincial distinctions and making everything of the most minute kind bend to what they call the good of the whole, is in other terms to say that these [Southern] colonies must be subject to the government of the Eastern provinces." His concern could not have been allayed by the terms of a draft of the Articles of Confederation which was submitted to the delegates by a special committee on July 12. This document, apparently because of the influence of John Dickinson of Pennsylvania, would have created a national legislature wielding great authority, except that its funds were to be supplied by requisitions upon the states. But that authority was sharply reduced by the body of delegates, with men from the South taking the lead in the making of the most significant change, the addition of a statement, "Each state retains its sovereignty, freedom, and independence, and every power, jurisdiction and right, which is not by this confederation expressly delegated to the United States in Congress assembled." North Carolinian Thomas Burke moved its inclusion, and the representatives of South Carolina seconded. Virginia gave the only vote against the change. Burke was apparently swayed principally by state allegience, as were the deputies from the North. It may reasonably be guessed that the South Carolinians were moved by larger considerations. Many other alterations were made which, taken together, lessened the powers of Congress until they were little more than those then exercised by the United States in the Pennsylvania State House.

Joining with their Northern colleagues in re-forming the Articles so that the national assembly became feeble rather than potentially tyrannical, the delegates from the South fought bitterly with those from the North over the apportionment of the costs of the central government among the states. The Congress had created a precedent in July, 1775, when it had declared that its paper currency was to be made good by the colonies in ratio to their respective numbers, including Negroes. The general committee's draft of the Articles similarly provided that the states would contribute to the national funds in proportion to inhabitants, Indians not taxed being not counted.

But the Southern delegates, realizing that their country was relatively much poorer, and that by this arrangement they would pay nearly half of the national expenses, demanded that it be modified; and a hot debate concerning apportionment began toward the close of July, 1776, and continued intermittently for several years. Samuel Chase of Maryland denounced the arrangement because, as he said, Negroes were property rather than persons—hence they should not be included in population. He offered an amending motion to that effect. John Adams, a Yankee satisfied with the system, tried to answer the Marylander. He said that a slave produced as much wealth as a white man—which was certainly not the fact— hence the Negroes should not be omitted. He was supported, more cogently, by James Wilson of Pennsylvania, who asserted that Chase's amendment would enable the Southerners to reap profit from slaves and would impose too heavy a burden upon the Northerners. Pointing out that Adams erred remarkably when he equated slave with white labor, Benjamin Harrison of Virginia declared that the labor of a white man was worth twice as much as that of a slave. Accordingly, he offered a compromise: that two Negroes should be counted as one white. This solution was acceptable to the Southerners, not to the Northerners. John Witherspoon of New Jersey, who saw that the Southerners had a case, then urged that the basis of apportionment be shifted from numbers to the value of private lands, together with improvements upon them. This scheme would have placed a relatively heavy burden upon the Northern states, especially those of New England, with its small and well kept farms. The Northern deputies insisted that donations be calculated according to the general committee's formula. Southerners more and more vigorously attacked it. It was useless to talk further about union, said Thomas Lynch of South Carolina, if it were not admitted that slaves were property. They were, and they were so taxed in South Carolina, said Lynch and Edward Rutledge. Rutledge, refusing to defend slavery as an institution, claimed it would be unfair to include Negroes in the formula, for their owners would be forced to contribute, while the proprietors of Northern merchant shipping, which must make great profits in carrying American goods as a result of union, would not be taxed therefor. William Hooper, a Yankee transplanted to North Carolina, properly pointed out that the formula was unfair to his state, which had a large population and relatively little wealth. All these arguments availed the Southerners nothing at the time. The Chase amendment was defeated, the sections lining up almost solidly in the balloting. New England and the Middle states, save for Delaware, voted nay; Georgia was divided, but the remainder of the South, with Delaware, voted aye.

This decision could not stand. Samuel Chase and

other delegates from Maryland openly declared that their state would never ratify the Articles of Confederation if it were not rescinded; and we may properly conclude that still other deputies from the Far South harbored similar sentiments. In 1777 the problem of dividing the burden of national expenses among the states was again debated. John Witherspoon's substitute formula calling for the use of lands and improvements thereupon was warmly discussed. The New Englanders were, as before, vigorously opposed to it. They wanted the Negroes included in any formula that might be adopted; and they had a new argument for doing so. A provision had been placed in the Articles calling for a Continental army with the states contributing men in ratio to their white inhabitants. The Yankees believed that recognition of the principle that the Negro was merely property would force them both to pay and to fight more than they equitably should. There was a belief among the Middle state delegates, however, that the South must be satisfied; and Witherspoon's formula was sanctioned by the Congress, Maryland, Virginia, the Carolinas, and New Jersey voting for it; Pennsylvania and New York splitting; and New England solidly voting in the negative.

The Witherspoon arrangement, endorsed by so narrow a margin, remained in the Articles of Confederation so long as that constitution endured. But Northern assaults upon it continued. The legislature of Connecticut, when the Articles were presented to the states for action in 1777, proposed an amendment which called for a return to the numbers-and-Negroes formula. It was promptly rejected by Congress, and Connecticut ratified the Articles without it. However, Southern and Northern states were equally remiss when it came to paying their quotas under the Witherspoon plan, for dollars were equally valued and difficult to secure on both sides of the Mason-Dixon line. The requisition system, as we all know, was a failure. Only too well aware that it must have substantial and reliable funds to operate, Congress in 1781 proposed an amendment which would have given it power to levy import duties. It failed to secure the unanimous approval of the states required by the Articles.

In 1783 the Congress again attacked its money problem, reviving the sectional quarrel over state contributions. On March 7, a Congressional committee on revenue brought before the delegates a proposed amendment which would have given

Congress authority to impose import duties for a period of twenty-five years—such duties being the most obvious and the simplest means of securing money. But the committee also called for the continuance of requisitions upon the states—contributing in ratio to numbers, including Negroes. The old quarrel was then resumed, with the Southerners again denouncing that scheme. Nor would they approve another, one offered by Pennsylvanian James Wilson, a $.25 per 100 acres tax on land—Southern soil was still less valuable than Northern. The committee on revenue revised its proposal: two Negroes should be counted as one white. This suggested compromise opened up a game of fractions on the floor of the house. Oliver Wolcott of Connecticut and Stephen Higginson of Massachusetts said four Negroes should be considered equal to three whites. Marylander Daniel Carroll would have it 4:1. John Rutledge thought 3:1 proper, but offered to accept 2:1. Other New Englanders supported 4:3. A motion for 3:2 was lost because all the Southern states voted against it. When solution seemed almost impossible, James Madison suggested 5:3, which Rutledge supported. Reconsidering, some Northern delegates then brought up 3:2, which was rejected. Madison had found the magic middle, and the amendment was framed accordingly. All the Southern states then represented, voted for it, and it was approved by the assemblies of Virginia and Maryland. But a majority of the states gave their consent only with clogging reservations; four of them did not even bother to reply yes or no; and it was accordingly defeated.

Other sectional issues appeared when the Articles of Confederation were examined by the state legislatures in 1777–1778. That of Virginia was alarmed lest the power of treaty-making vested in Congress lead to a bargain which would give New England special advantages in carrying Southern products, although it finally decided that the danger was remote. Those of New Jersey and Pennsylvania proposed an amendment which would have settled state quotas for the Continental army on the basis of total numbers rather than white numbers. The assembly of Georgia wished to alter the "privileges and immunities" clause so that it would definitely not apply to Negroes. (Georgia also would have excluded pacifists and traitors.)

It was South Carolina, partly because of the influence of William Henry Drayton, that exhibited sectionalism in greatest vigor, indeed in a degree and manner prophetic of the history of that state during the years 1828-1860. On January 14, 1778, its assembly informed Governor John Rutledge that the question of ratifying the Articles was "stupendously important, and ought to be maturely digested and equally weighed, and critically examined. We shall enter upon consideration of this business with minds perfectly disposed to a confederated union of the states, upon a principle of equality, delegating only as much of our sovereignty as may be absolutely necessary for the general safety. It is obvious that the legislature was fearful of the tyranny of a central government; it is not surprising, therefore, that it gave heed to Drayton, who offered to it his own draft of a constitution in lieu of the Articles. He believed that the Articles gave far too much authority to Congress, and that its power would be exerted to the disadvantage of the South, unless constitutional safeguards were established. He would withhold from Congress "any power, that can with propriety, be exercised by the several states—or any power, but what is clearly defined beyond a doubt." Moreover, he was profoundly concerned because the Articles required the consent of only nine state delegations when Congress made use of its few major powers.

When I reflect, that from the nature of the climate, soil and produce of the several states, a northern and southern interest in many particulars naturally and unavoidably rise; I cannot but be displeased with the prospect, that the most important transactions in Congress, may be done contrary to the united opposition of Virginia, the two Carolinas and Georgia; states possessing more than one half of the whole territory of the confederacy; and forming, as I may say, the body of the southern interest . . . the honor, interest and sovereignty of the south, are in effect delivered up to the care of the north. Do we intend to make such a surrender?

Drayton asserted that he did not fear the North, but nevertheless demanded that all the important business of Congress require the consent of eleven state delegations. Accordingly, Congress would not be able to declare war, make peace, agree to a treaty, or do anything of great consequence without the consent of half of the states Drayton considered to be Southern. He did not insist upon concurrent sectional majorities, although he went far in that direction, especially since he did not consider Maryland to be Southern. Quite logically, he also would have it that future amendments should become effective when approved by eleven states.

Now it was well known in South Carolina that Drayton was a man who took pride in his education, completed in England, and that he was fond of intellectual dispute, given to fine points of logic. Nor did he have an unassailable reputation for consistency, since he was an ardent and outspoken champion of British authority before he became a Patriot leader. Some men in the assembly must have doubted that serious sectional controversy was so certain, that Congress under the Articles could become a truly effective engine for Northern tyranny. Nevertheless, Drayton had shown ability and zeal as a Patriot, and his arguments had effect. Setting aside his personal constitution, the assembly proposed amendments to the Articles based upon it, including his proviso that the votes of eleven states should be necessary for the conduct of important business in Congress and for future changes in the Articles. It also urged, like the Georgia legislature, that Negroes be specifically excluded from the benefits of the "privileges and immunities" clause.

There followed anticlimax. Receiving many proposed amendments to the Articles from the states, the Congress in 1778 rejected all of them. The two principal ones offered by South Carolina received only two affirmative votes, doubtless those of South Carolina and Georgia. It is most unlikely that they received Virginia or North Carolina support, since both of those Southern states had ratified the Articles without reservation. Would South Carolina insist upon having her way? She did not, but instead bowed to a demand by Congress that she approve the Articles without exception. That South Carolina abandoned the contest may be explained in part by the fact that Drayton had been elected a member of Congress and had departed from the local scene. In Congress, it will be recalled, he favored the enlistment of slaves as soldiers, but his stand on that issue does not indicate that he had abandoned his sectional fears. At Philadelphia he was with respect to other issues an ardent champion of Southern interests. He died there in 1779. We may wonder, had he lived, whether the course of history in South Carolina might have been different from what it was.

In Congress, Drayton, with the other deputies, began to consider early in 1779 what goals the United States should strive to achieve at the peace table, since it was then believed that French intervention might soon bring the war to a close; and he and they slipped into another harassing sectional controversy. The delegates agreed that recognition of independence and as generous boundaries as possible must be secured. However, when they began to discuss the Newfoundland fisheries and the Mississippi River, free use of both being desired by all, New Englanders insisted that it was far more important to obtain the right to fish on the Grand Banks than it was to get freedom of navigation on the Father of Waters; conversely, most of the Southerners, including Drayton, believed that unrestricted use of the great river was vital, while the right to catch cod was only desirable. Fishing on the Grand Banks put large sums of money into Yankee pocketbooks; on the other hand, the right to traverse the Mississippi (including the use of port facilities at or near New Orleans) seemed to most Southerners, particularly those of Virginia and North Carolina, essential to the expansion of the Southern states and necessary to permit the marketing of products soon to be ready for export from the settlements of Kentucky and Tennessee. The New Englanders wanted access to the fisheries to be made a *sine qua non;* the champions of the South sought the same status for use of the river. Each group fancied that the other asked too much.

In February, 1779, as a result, there began a

contest over cod which endured for six months. Among the Southerners only Richard Henry Lee of Virginia and Henry Laurens of South Carolina were willing to join the Yankees in pushing hard for the American right to cast nets off Newfoundland; and some of the delegates from the Middle states sided with the majority of the men from the South. The result was a stalemate in terms of votes. Recriminations abounded in debate; compromises which would in effect have given the victory to one group or the other were offered, correctly analyzed, and then defeated. Sectional feeling ran high in Congress and then spread across the nation; and Lee and Laurens were bitterly assailed by Southern colleagues. Lee escaped abuse when he temporarily retired to private life, but Laurens was less fortunate. Whitmell Hill, delegate from North Carolina, described Laurens as a "Southern champion" easily "duped by their flattery, an artillery which he cannot oppose."

Laurens, although he doubtless voted for what he thought to be the general good, was the more vigorously attacked because he was the key figure in the struggle. He and Drayton then formed the delegation of South Carolina; and the Southern faction lost the vote of that state because Laurens and Drayton canceled each other out. Drayton and Laurens engaged in oral, written, and nasty controversy; and Laurens was also assailed by the entire North Carolina delegation, Whitmell Hill, Thomas Burke, and John Penn. Encouraged by Drayton, they wrote Laurens an abusive and threatening letter. How could South Carolina support the Yankees in their demand for the use of the fisheries as a *sine qua non* and so perhaps prolong the war? Wasn't South Carolina weak in men and resources? If such was not the case, she had deceived her sister state, which had been forced to come to her aid against the British enemy. They threatened, if Laurens did not change his vote, to ask the governor of North Carolina to withdraw North Carolina troops from South Carolina and to keep them at home. Returning sneer for sneer, Laurens assailed both Drayton and the men from the "Land of Turpentine." Refusing to be cowed, he demanded that the North Carolinians withdraw their threat. They did not quite dare to execute it, and the quarrel died down.

At last the fight between the Yankees and the Southern faction over fishing also came to an end, because the New Englanders abandoned it. Rather than continue to wrestle in the hall of Congress, they consented on August 14 to making the use of the fisheries a desirable goal in the peace negotiations, but not a *sine qua non*. They hoped, however, that the Patriot emissaries who asserted the interests of the United States would not too weakly defend those of New England.

The Mississippi River question was a source of discord between North and South even longer than the fisheries dispute, indeed until the Louisiana Purchase gave the United States control of the lower reaches of the great river. In one form or another, with additions and subtractions, it created much bitter feeling during the decade 1779–1789. When Congress first began to consider the Southern demand that free use of the river be secured, Spain, which owned both its banks just above its mouth, was still a neutral. Moreover, the Southerners wanted to seize the Floridas, which were still held by the British, but which were coveted also by Spain. William Henry Drayton and Thomas Burke tried to make the opening of the river a *sine qua non* in the peace negotiations, but a motion to that effect, considered on March 24, 1779, encountered heavy opposition. The two Carolinians tried to soften it by pushing an amendment which stipulated that the *sine qua non* was to be abandoned if

America's allies were unable to continue the war. To no avail, for both the motion and the amendment were defeated by heavy votes, although many delegates conceded that the right to navigate the river was desirable and that the Floridas would be valuable acquisitions. In the following September a bargain was worked out, after M. Conrad Alexandre Gérard, the first French minister to the United States, had pointed out that Congress could expect no help from Spain against Britain if it insisted upon getting both the Floridas and the free use of the river. That body accordingly undertook to give up all claim to the two provinces below the 31st parallel, and to help Spain take them from Britain in return for the right of navigation.

By that time Spain had entered the war, not as an American ally, but as a French one, seeking especially to regain Gibraltar, but keenly interested also in the Floridas, they being valued as barrier colonies to protect the Spanish possessions in Mexico and the Caribbean. John Jay of New York, sent to Madrid to push for the bargain proposed by Congress, was long unable even to secure a hearing at the Spanish court. Meanwhile, the Spanish began the conquest of West Florida; and the whole question was again debated in Congress in November,

1780. Two delegates from Georgia, George Walton and Richard Howley, announced that they were willing to give up the effort to obtain the use of the river in order to make sure of other gains. They urged that Congress agree to abandon both that right and all territory west of the Mobile River to Spain in exchange for a loan and a promise by the government of Charles III not to oppose American interests in the peace negotiations. This proposition would have left East Florida open to Georgian expansion, it may be observed. The delegation of Virginia, the state most interested in opening up the river, promptly protested, and the Georgia scheme was as quickly defeated. But the Virginians were not so dominated by selfish wishes that they would make no sacrifice to the common good. James Madison was well aware that Spanish good will might help to achieve American independence; that even if it were achieved without the aid of the dons, Spain could with Britain cause embarrassment for the United States, especially in the Southwest. He persuaded his fellow delegates from the Old Dominion and also the Virginia assembly to announce that they would consent to abandoning the attempt to secure navigation of the Mississippi, if necessary to secure the good will and help of Spain. Congress was then able, on February 15, 1781, to send new orders to John Jay telling him he could use the right of navigation as a bargaining point.

So Virginia conceded on the river question as New England had softened on the fishing question. Moreover, when choosing commissioners to negotiate the peace treaty, Congress carefully selected men from all parts of the confederation, John Adams of Massachusetts, John Jay of New York, Benjamin Franklin of Pennsylvania, Thomas Jefferson of Virginia, and Henry Laurens of South Carolina. As it happened, the neat balance of this delegation was destroyed by events. Laurens was captured at sea by the British and kept as a prisoner in the Tower of London until the treaty with Britain was well advanced. Jefferson, because of the last illness and death of his wife, declined to serve, much to the distress of at least one Virginian, Edmund Randolph, who scolded Jefferson because his refusal left "Southern interests" without a Southern champion in the delegation. Thus the South was not represented by a Southerner at Paris. The South lost nothing as a result. Jay, after receiving contemptuous treatment at Madrid, became profoundly distrustful of the intentions of both Spain and France toward the United States and behaved accordingly in the French capital. The American emissaries did all they could for the United States. It was not possible for them to secure the Floridas, or either of them, or Spanish consent to the right of navigation, or an unquestionable right to exploit the Grand Banks fisheries.

Although Franklin, Adams, and Jay strove to achieve the wishes of both the South and New England, Southerners continued to demand representation at foreign courts after the close of the war. Virginians in and out of Congress, in 1784, insisted that Southern interests be taken into account in choosing new ministers to European countries. They were satisfied by the appointment of Jefferson as envoy to France. But Virginians and other Southerners in Congress continued to find fault with the Yankee deputies on other grounds. That same year Richard Dobbs Spaight of North Carolina said concerning them:

> Since I have had the honor of a seat in Congress their uniform conduct has been to weaken the power of the union as much as possible, and sacrifice our national strength and dignity in hopes of rendering themselves more conspicuous and individual states . . . I do not think they wish for a

dissolution of the Confederacy, but they press so extremely hard on the chain that unites us, that I imagine it will break before they are well aware of it. A separation certainly would not be to their advantage. . . . This event may by many be thought to be distant, but it is my opinion that unless those states lay aside their present policy, and adopt one more liberal . . . it will happen in a very short period.

Moreover, the Mississippi question continued to exasperate. Spain, letting the Americans pass up and down the river until 1784, declared it closed to them in that year. The United States, claiming that the right of navigation had been inherited from the British (who had secured it in the Peace of Paris of 1763), vigorously protested. From the West and from Virginia came violent denunciations of Spain on this account and others. Kentuckians asserted that they had a natural right to use the river. If they were barred from it, they must eventually use force; some of them hinted they would declare their independence or even join hands with the Spanish in order to open the river, unless Virginia and the United States moved decisively. In Virginia feeling was almost as strong, although Richard Henry Lee and Washington did not believe the right of navigation was immediately important to the state. Washington, indeed, believed that everything possible should be done instead to establish transportation routes across the Appalachians between Virginia and the West. Were they not soon built, he feared that the West would be lost to Virginia and the United States.

Strangely enough, the excitement of the Kentuckians and Virginians in the 1780's was caused by anticipation of economic troubles rather than actual ones, for the Kentuckians had little to export until after 1789. This fact seemed important to John Jay, secretary for foreign affairs, when Don Diego de Gardoqui came to Philadelphia in 1785 as a Spanish chargé d'affaires to try to negotiate a Spanish-American agreement. It did not seem very important to Congress, which instructed Jay to make no concession concerning use of the river and also to insist upon the American version of the disputed boundary between the United States and Spanish West Florida. After many months of fruitless discussion with Gardoqui, Jay concluded that he could not secure commercial concessions from Spain, which he keenly desired, unless the United States softened its stand upon the river question. Accordingly, he asked Congress to permit him to concede to Spain full control over the Mississippi for twenty-five years.

Jay's request caused a storm in Congress. Men from New England and the Middle States heartily agreed with him that the right of navigation was of no great immediate importance. They were all the more disposed to see eye-to-eye with him because they were not eager to foster Southern expansion; indeed, some of them were keenly opposed to such expansion. James Monroe, then a delegate from Virginia, believed that they were such determined enemies of the growth of settlements below the Ohio that they would prefer to leave the confederation and to form a new one north of the Mason-Dixon line rather than permit it. If they made such an attempt, he would want a Southern confederacy; and Pennsylvania must be part of it, brought in by force if necessary. Patrick Henry's sentiments were equally violent—Madison later reported that it was principally the Northern attitude regarding the Mississippi question that persuaded Henry not to accept appointment to the Philadelphia Convention of 1787. Despite the vigor of the objections of Southerners inside Congress and out, the delegates from the North insisted upon giving Jay the authority he requested. In September, 1786, a motion permitting him to waive the right of navigation for twenty-five years and also to make boundary concessions, if necessary, was carried by seven states to five, the South voting solidly against it, seven Northern states voting solidly for it, Delaware not being represented. So the South lost a very hot engagement, but not a war. A treaty with Spain could not be approved without the consent of nine delegations in Congress; and Jay sensibly refrained from trying to use the power which had been given to him. The river question was finally passed on to the new federal government in 1789.[1]

In view of the sectional troubles which arose during the War of Independence and continued into the period of the Confederation, it is not surprising that the proposed admission of new states also caused sectional dissension. Southern opposition helped to prevent the admission of Vermont;

[1] Southern resentment over the Mississippi question was not confined to Virginia. Reported Timothy Bloodworth, North Carolina delegate, to Richard Caswell on September 29, 1786: ". . . the utmost warmth appeared on this occasion from each party . . . and the majority appears determined to carry on the treaty at all events and the minority as firmly fixed to oppose it . . . For my own part I think the precedent dangerous to the liberties of the Southern states if seven states can barter any part of the privileges of the different states

and Northerners became concerned as it became ever more likely that Kentucky would seek to be recognized as a state. These questions would become acute, of course, only if other sectional disputes were genuinely serious. Moreover, a solution was available: the admission of both states.

Nor should there be surprise, in view of those troubles, that there was clash between North and South regarding the location of the American capital before 1789. As early as June, 1775, there was sectional difference of opinion regarding the place where Congress should meet. It was several times unofficially proposed by members that it move from Philadelphia to Hartford or New Haven so as to be near the scene of military action at that time. Joseph Hewes, delegate from North Carolina, reporting on this proposal, declared that "some of the Southern gentlemen have not yet given their consent, nor do I think they ever will." Nor did

---

for any advantages whatsoever, there remains no security for any possession. It is well known that the balance of power is now in the Eastern states, and they appear determined to keep it in that direction."

In November, 1787, the Virginia House of Delegates went so far as to demand that Congress acknowledge it lacked power either to "cede or suspend" the right of Virginians to use the river.

the Southern members ever agree to meetings in New England. On the other hand, Northern members certainly did not desire sessions in the Far South. During the war the Congress continued to meet at Philadelphia and other locations in the Middle states.

At the close of the conflict the question of a permanent residence inevitably came before Congress; and almost as inevitably it aroused contention. In October, 1783, formal debates began. It quickly became apparent that the New Englanders wanted the capital located as far to the northward as possible; Pennsylvania, New York, New Jersey, and Delaware wished to place it on the Delaware River; Maryland was determined to have it at Annapolis; Virginia favored Georgetown; and the Far South urged that it be placed as far to the southward as possible. Convenience, economic advantage, and sectional prides and jealousies affected views and results. So Hugh Williamson, of North Carolina, contending for a location at the falls of the Potomac, said that the capital should not be placed "on a corner of the empire," that the center of population was moving southward and westward, that the location he championed would add to the "honor and prosperity of the Southern

states." A spot on the Hudson, supported by the
New Englanders, was voted down. It was then proposed, on October 7, 1783, that "buildings for the
use of Congress be erected on or near the banks of
the Delaware." A motion to that effect was carried
by a strictly sectional vote, all the seven Northern
states represented saying aye, all the four Southern
states represented saying nay. But that decision did
not stand, because the Delaware delegates had
voted as they did only because they had hoped that
the choice would fall upon Wilmington. It soon
became apparent that a location on the Delaware
River meant Trenton, not Wilmington. The Delaware deputies preferred the Potomac as their second choice. As a result, when Hugh Williamson
moved for reconsideration on the following day so
as to reach a solution which "shall approach nearer
to that justice which is due to the Southern states,"
Delaware voted with the solid South, but the motion was lost by 6 votes to 5. The question could
not moderately be decided by so close a margin.
Accordingly, on October 20, Elbridge Gerry of
Massachusetts moved for a compromise, the establishment of two capitals to be used alternately, the
one on the Delaware, the other on the Potomac.
This resolution was sanctioned 7 to 1, New Eng-

land and the South carrying it against the opposition of the Middle states. On the following day, the Congress resolved to meet temporarily and alternately at Trenton and Annapolis. But this decision also failed to stand, for delegates from the Far South had lost interest in supporting Southern claims—after all, New York was more accessible for them than either Trenton or Annapolis; and the Congress accordingly moved to the northward, to New York in 1785. The question of permanent location was, of course, to be revived in 1789.

If, in the years 1785–1786, when economic depression afflicted the entire Confederation, Southerners were unhappy because Northerners were lukewarm or hostile to Southern expansion, Northerners were discontented because Southerners were neutral toward or opposed to measures which would have benefited the maritime trade of the North. Merchants of New England and the Middle states wanted protection for their shipping against British competition, especially after Parliament decided to treat the Americans as foreigners and applied the British navigation laws to them. Accordingly, New England sought to amend the Articles of Confederation so as to give Congress powers to regulate interstate and foreign commerce and to levy import and export duties toward that end. Even though the proceeds of these taxes were to go to the states in which they were collected and the power to cut off commerce was expressly reserved to them, Southerners in Congress, especially Virginians, objected strenuously. Members of the Virginia legislature also evidently protested. They feared that Congress would use these powers to prevent British ships from coming to Southern shores and so to confer upon Northern shipowners a monopoly of the Southern overseas traffic. Certainly the Yankees wished to get as much of that business as they could; and American shipping was concentrated in the Northern ports, being relatively scarce in the Southern ones. Washington, as usual, took a broad and conciliatory stand. When James McHenry of Maryland wrote to the General to express his alarm, Washington replied that he was quite willing to give Congress the authority, which could not be exercised without the votes of nine states:

> . . . let the Southern states always be represented; let them act more in union; let them declare freely and boldly what is for the interest of, and what is prejudiced to their constituents; and there

will, there *must* be an accommodating spirit; in the establishment of a navigation act, this in a particular manner ought, and will doubtless be attended to. If the assent of nine (or as some propose, of eleven states, is necessary to give validity to a commercial system; it insures this measure, or it cannot be obtained. . . . I confess to you candidly, that I can forsee no evil greater than disunion than those *unreasonable* jealousies . . . which are continually poisoning our minds and filling them with imaginary evils to the prevention of real ones.

In any case, said Washington, if the New Englanders secured the Southern carrying trade because the British were barred from it and because Southerners could not successfully compete for it with the Yankees, it was certainly better that the Yankees should secure it at the expense of the British, who injured America at every opportunity. James Madison, who was in Congress, also was disposed to make a concession to the Northern shipowners. But the remainder of the Virginia delegation was hostile, and there was opposition among other Southern deputies. The amendment therefore died in Congress; and a substitute which would have given that body severely limited authority over navigation was approved, but was neglected by the state legislatures, especially those of the Far South. Indeed, by 1786, it had become seemingly impossible to make changes in the Articles of Confederation, these requiring both action by Congress and the sanction of all thirteen state legislatures. Certainly, sectional antagonism was a special and difficult stumbling block, as Madison ruefully observed. In August of that year when James Monroe reported that New Englanders were considering the formation of a separate union, he was not entirely in error. Wrote Yankee Theodore Sedgwick on the 6th of that month:

> It well becomes the eastern and middle states, who are in interest one, seriously to consider what advantages result to them from their connection with the Southern states. They can give us nothing, as an equivalent for the protection which they desire from us but a participation in their commerce. This they deny to us. Should their conduct continue the same . . . an attempt to perpetuate our connection with them, which at last too will be found ineffectual, will sacrifice everything to a meer chimera. Even the appearance of a union cannot in the way we now are long be preserved. It becomes us seriously to contemplate a substitute.

But the forces of nationalism were powerful in New England, and also in the South. Within two years the Yankees and the Southerners were to establish, with the Middle Americans, a stronger union.

(3)

The South and the Making of the Constitution

In the light of what has been said about basic sources of conflict between South and North and about the conflicts which actually took place during the years 1774–1787, it may well be asked: why did the Southerners help to make the Constitution of 1787, and why did they ratify it in their state conventions, so joining in the creation of a far more powerful central government and so presumably enlarging the risk of Northern tyranny? Toward answering these questions, it should be recalled that Northerners were not yet attacking the institution of slavery in the South, and that it was unnecessary for Southerners to defend it. It should also be remembered that the conflicts of the years 1774–1787 were not all settled in favor of the North; there had been Southern victories as well as Northern ones, and compromises too. Nor should it be forgotten that it was possible to establish a strong central government, and at the same time to limit its authority at specific points where Southerners feared it would act seriously against Southern interests. Moreover, just at the time when the Constitution was made and ratified, in the years 1787–1788, it seemed to many Southerners— who were perhaps eager to believe such was the case—that the South was growing more rapidly than the North. At that time there was a rush of Northern farmers to the Southern interior, which did not, as it happened, long endure; just then, Kentucky and Tennessee were growing rapidly; just then, the Old Northwest was still Indian country, its first settlement, Marietta, Ohio, being founded only in 1788. It could plausibly be asserted and even reasonably be believed that the South would not only be able to hold her own at the national capital but to dominate it. There was also the fact that the first powerful single executive at the national capital could hardly be other than the man of Mount Vernon. There were still other reasons why Southerners, like Northerners, wanted a stronger union: disgust caused by bickering among the states; the feeling of nationalism, including a desire for national dignity; the need for more effective military forces against the Indians and European nations; and the economic benefits which such a union could hardly fail to bring to all Americans.

Moreover, there were special reasons why some very influential Southerners, like some very influential Northerners, pushed for a strong central government. These were the so-called Conservatives who believed that the Revolution had gone too far, or threatened to go too far. Tidewater merchants, planters, lawyers, and clergymen, and others, they had, with the British, rather effectively dominated the American political scene before 1775; they had hoped to inherit that share of authority formerly wielded by the British; instead, they had been defeated by factions composed of Liberals and Democrats at some state capitals and were in danger of defeat at others. They might be able to reverse the tide by transferring power to a central government and by making constitutional arrangements which would enable them to control it. Moreover, the Conservatives were swayed toward such a government by economic considerations. Some of them held certificates of indebtedness, those famous promises to pay which had been issued by the central regime. They were currently at a heavy discount. A financially responsible central government might well choose to redeem them at par, paying back those patriotic Americans who had accepted the papers in return for solid values in order to help the cause against Britain, and also rewarding those shrewd Americans who had bought the certificates at discount from the original holders. Besides, the power of issuing paper money might be exclusively placed in Congress. Thus the state legislatures could be denied a practice which had become popular in them, the putting forth of quantities of cheap paper with legal tender quality which debtors used to pay off obligations contracted in hard money—cheap paper which fluctuated in value and unsettled economic transactions generally.

There were, then, generally pervasive forces and also special forces which made possible an ultimately successful drive for the creation of a stronger union. They made themselves felt when the Annapolis Convention of 1786, under the guidance of Alexander Hamilton and James Madison, with the blessing of Washington, issued invitations to the states to send delegates to a convention in Philadelphia "to devise such further provisions as shall appear to them necessary to render the constitution of the federal government adequate to the exigencies of the union; and to report such an act for that purpose to the United States in Congress assembled, as, when agreed to by them, and afterwards confirmed by the legislatures of every state, will effectually provide for the same." The response of the American public was so generally favorable that the Congress, although some of its members did not like the scheme of a special constitutional convention, made the invitation official in February, 1787. Moreover, every state except Rhode Island responded by sending men to Philadelphia.

The South was well represented at Philadelphia in that famous body which finally produced *the* Constitution at the end of the summer of that year. As it happened, Maryland did not send her best men, who remained at home, partly to fight against a paper money scheme, partly because they lacked hope that the Convention would accomplish anything. Her spokesmen were Daniel Carroll, Daniel of St. Thomas Jenifer, John Francis Mercer, James McHenry, and Luther Martin, who were of the middle order of politicians, without towering talents. Luther Martin was the most talkative of the group; he was not remarkable for constructive ability. North Carolina was represented by a similar delegation, William Blount, William R. Davie, Alexander Martin, Richard Dobbs Spaight, and Dr. Hugh Williamson. Williamson had more to say than the other North Carolinians; like Martin, he was not a principal architect of the Constitution. Nor were the gentlemen from Georgia, Abraham Baldwin, William Few, William Houstoun, and William Pierce, very distinguished. It was otherwise with the South Carolinians, Pierce Butler, Charles Pinckney, Charles Cotesworth Pinckney, and John Rutledge. Butler's abilities were apparently no more than respectable. Charles Pinckney's talents were of a somewhat higher order. The son of a Tory planter, he was liberal-minded, unafraid of change. He was to be useful in the Convention in helping to solve problems of detail. C. C. Pinckney was a superior man, courageous, trustworthy, and amiable. Rutledge was the leading lawyer and politician of South Carolina, also remarkably reliable. As governor of the state he had staunchly persevered in defending it against the British. The South Carolinians, all except Charles Pinckney being of a Conservative complexion, formed a group of able men who were devoted to the interests of their state but who were also friendly to the concept of a stronger union. They

did not match in genius—nor did the delegation of
any other state—the Virginians, John Blair, Dr.
James McClurg, Madison, George Mason, Edmund
Randolph, George Wythe, and Washington. Blair
and McClurg were not great upon the public
scene, and Randolph was as important because of
his membership in the Randolph clan as he was for
his genius. Wythe and Mason were enlightened lawyers, Mason a champion of personal liberty. They
would have been leaders of the first rank in any
other delegation; in that of Virginia they were
overshadowed by the majestic figure of Washington and little Mr. Madison. The General presided
stiffly over the Convention, and said few words
about the issues which it faced. He was not quick-
witted, and he did not pretend to know every pre-
cise answer to every awkward problem. He was,
however, the very personification of American na-
tionality, and no one in the Pennsylvania State
House could doubt that he desired any necessary
sacrifice of personal or regional interest toward the
founding of a strong and permanent union. Nor
could anyone question his affection for Mount
Vernon and Virginia. Madison, solicitous for Virginia, was also sturdily intent upon making a stout
and stable central government. He was fertile in de-

vising machinery for it, and equally fertile in finding means to soften jarring jealousies. It has often been said that he was the Father of the Constitution. He was its progenitor more than any other man with respect to specifics. But was not Washington its chief sponsor, at least its godparent?

Reaching Philadelphia early, the Virginia men had time to discuss among themselves the problems to be faced by the Convention. They ended by preparing the Virginia Plan, often called the Madison Plan, because Madison was doubtless its principal draftsman. It did not contain a proposed list of amendments to the Articles of Confederation, but described a new constitution and a powerful central government. Indeed, that government was to be given such vast authority that it is difficult to believe that all the Virginia delegates approved of it wholeheartedly; and it may well be that even Madison and Washington were not actually prepared to go so far toward concentration of power at the federal capital as the Plan indicated. It called for a Congress of two houses, the lower one elected directly by the voters, with representation based on wealth or numbers, the members of the upper house chosen by those of the lower. The legislature would choose the executive. A national judiciary would have power to decide cases involving "the national peace and harmony." The Congress was to have remarkably large powers. They could not have been further increased without reducing the states to a completely inferior position. The Congress was to have all the powers it possessed under the Articles. It was also to be authorized to legislate in all areas when the "separate states" were "incompetent," also in those where state activity might threaten the harmony of the union. Still further, it was to be able to set aside state laws violating the national constitution, and was to be authorized to use force against any state "failing to fulfill its duty." In sum, this Congress would virtually be the judge of its own powers with reference to the states.

It should startle that the Virginians not only prepared this plan, but offered it to the Convention. They could hardly have expected that it would basically be accepted. Yet both they and other Southern delegates, as well as Northern ones, were obviously prepared to go far toward concentration of power in the central government. That was true even of the South Carolinians, if the special interests of the Low Country were suitably protected, as they would presently demonstrate. It

was also true of the Georgia men and of the North
Carolinians, if the special interests of their states,
similar to those of South Carolina, were safe-
guarded against action by a heedless Northern majority in control of the central government.

In the Convention the Virginia Plan was made
the basis for discussion. One great decision was
quickly made, to draw up a new Constitution
rather than to try to amend the Articles of Confederation. Then, as all students of American history are aware, the delegates engaged in a furious
struggle between the "large" and "small" states, a
conflict which was not sectional in nature, which
was not even based on political realities (for the
Founding Fathers were not always so wise as we
are accustomed to believe). Men from the "small"
states, jealous of their larger neighbors, feared that
they would combine to control the central government, and that they would be able to do so if its
power was exercised by men chosen on the basis of
numbers or wealth. Mr. Madison intelligently said
that such men would be moved by economic and
regional interests, not by the proportions of the
states in which they resided, to no purpose. It was
necessary to placate the "small" state party, and
that was achieved by the so-called "Great Com-

promise" or "Connecticut Compromise," the latter
term indicating the important role in making it
played by the men from the Nutmeg State. The
same men, perhaps pleased by their statesman-
ship and their importance in finding a solution to
this quarrel, were again to find middle ground
when major difficulties arose between North and
South.

That there would be sectional quarrels in the
Convention had to be assumed. As Madison afterward reported, no Southern delegate spoke in favor
of creating a separate confederacy below the
Mason-Dixon line. Nevertheless, many men from
the South, including Madison himself, sought with
varying vehemence to make sure that the South
would not suffer seriously by helping to create a
stronger union. George Mason, early in the debates,
proposed a triple executive of men from New England, the Middle states, and the South, so as to
ensure that the South would always have a share
(perhaps possessing even a veto) in the control of
the executive branch. One is reminded of John C.
Calhoun's scheme of 1850 for two Presidents, one
Northern and the other Southern. Later on, Hugh
Williamson indicated that he favored Mason's proposal, but it was opposed by Charles Pinckney and

John Rutledge. The two South Carolinians apparently believed that the protection of Southern interests did not require such a safeguard. They could believe that a single executive, even one from New England or the Middle states, would not necessarily be hostile to the South; he would at times probably be a Southerner; the first one could hardly be other than a Southerner, Washington.

Far more serious to the delegates from the South was the matter of the basis of representation in the lower house. Toward settling that problem, James Wilson of Pennsylvania suggested on June 11 that apportionment be made according to the number of free men, counting slaves as three-fifths and excluding Indians not taxed. This was, of course, the formula which Madison had suggested as a compromise with respect to state support of the Confederation in 1783; and it was approved by the Convention with little debate. But delegates would not permit so swift a solution. Three weeks later Gouverneur Morris, a stout Conservative, called for reconsideration of the problem. He wanted to base representation upon riches as well as numbers. Declared he: "Life and liberty were generally said to be of more value, than property. An accurate view of the matter would nevertheless prove that property was the main object of society." This was talk that appealed to South Carolina aristocrats, and Pierce Butler, C. C. Pinckney, and Rutledge gave hearty support to Morris' proposal. They believed that their wealth in slaves would give South Carolina a large representation. They fancied that slaves could be counted both as property and as persons. The result was the appointment of a special committee, its membership including Morris and Rutledge, which recommended on July 9 that both wealth and numbers be taken into account, with the Congress establishing the representation of new states upon those bases.

By this scheme it would have been possible for the Congress to discriminate seriously against new states to be formed west of the Appalachians, exactly as the Low Country aristocrats were accustomed to discriminate against the Upcountry people in South Carolina, who were then grossly under-represented by numbers. So the wealthy East could keep down the poorer and perhaps ultimately more populous West. But so also the North would be able to limit the growth of Southern representation, specifically in Kentucky and Tennessee; and Morris and other Northern delegates who favored this plan undoubtedly had *that* in mind. Madison, seeing clearly what was in the thoughts of the Northerners and in those of the Low Country aristocrats, pushed for a scheme which was both more democratic and intended to protect the Southern interest. He proposed and secured a provision requiring a periodic census, with apportionment based upon the numbers thereby discovered.

Madison could hardly have succeeded in destroying the wealth plus population formula, had its sponsors been united. But the South Carolinians had become well aware that Morris had no intention of permitting the counting of slaves in both categories. Indeed, it being decided that numbers were to be the yardstick, both Morris and William Paterson contended that the slaves should not be counted at all. C. C. Pinckney talked, not very accurately, about "the superior wealth" of the Far South and insisted it must be given due weight, and Pierce Butler spoke to the same effect. They wanted the slaves counted equally with the free. The three-fifths formula was accordingly threatened. A motion to count the Negroes with the whites received only the votes of South Carolina, Georgia, and Delaware, with men from the Upper South—these obviously standing by the compro-

mise fraction—joining those of the North to defeat it. The Northerners then put and carried a
motion that the three-fifths formula be scrapped,
and it was carried, on July 11, by six states to four.
Virginia, North Carolina, and Georgia voted nay.
So did Connecticut, because the Connecticut delegation believed that the compromise was essential.
South Carolina voted with the Northerners, but to
insist upon counting the Negroes, whereas they
voted as they did to exclude the Negroes. The
three-fifths formula was thus set aside, but was it?
The following day North Carolina's William R.
Davie, usually silent, made it clear that Morris,
Paterson, and their followers could not have their
way. He said North Carolina "would never confederate on any terms that did not rate them [the
slaves] at least as $\frac{3}{5}$. If the Eastern states meant,
therefore, to exclude them altogether the business
was at an end."

It had become evident that the North must concede ground. Realizing that such was the situation,
Morris came forth with a motion that "direct taxation shall be in proportion to representation."
Thus the greater the representation of the South
because of the counting of the slaves, the greater
would be the direct taxes imposed upon the South-

ern states. The Southern delegates could not logically oppose the motion, and they did not. Nor
could the Northern men then contend against the
three-fifths ratio for representation. The formula
was accordingly established, with general approval,
both for representation and for direct taxation.
The South was to lose little by the concession with
regard to direct taxes, since they were seldom imposed by Congress.

Other sectional issues had already appeared, and
more were to come. The Convention had to appor-
tion members for the first House of Representatives under the Constitution. A committee drew
up a plan giving the Northern states 36 representatives, the Southern states only 29. There was objection from the Far Southern men. They tried to
secure more representatives for South Carolina and
Georgia and to reduce the number for New
Hampshire, but they failed. Madison fought
against the equal representation of the states in
the Senate because he feared that the South might
be in the minority in that body, but he could make
no great impression, particularly because the
smaller states were determined to have equality in
the upper house with the larger ones. Madison also
urged the appointment of federal judges with the

consent of two-thirds of the Senate. He was opposed to approval by a simple majority. Were
merely a majority required, judges might be ap-
pointed who were satisfactory only to a Northern
minority of the American population. Such hap-
penings would supply "a perpetual ground of
jealousy and discontent . . . to the Southern states."
He failed to secure his point. Other Southerners
sought to protect Southern interests at other
points. Some of them vigorously urged that treaties should be approved by two-thirds of the senators present, rather than by a simple majority.
Behind this demand lay the now only too familiar
Mississippi question. The Southerners wanted
neither the cession of territory in the Southwest
nor of the right of navigation by a Northern president supported by a plain Senate majority. The
demand aroused sympathy among Northern delegates who feared lest a Southern president, backed
by a simple Senate majority, barter away Northern
interests. The two-thirds provision regarding treaties was accordingly inserted in the Constitution.

Sectionalism also appeared when the Convention
had to decide whether to give Congress authority
in general terms, as did the Virginia Plan, or to list
its powers in detail. The delegates from the Far

South would sanction a general statement only if Congress were specifically forbidden to act against slavery and to levy export taxes. They preferred to have both enumerated powers and the prohibitions, toward securing as solid protection as possible against national action hostile to the Far South. Since there was widespread among all the delegates the fear that Congress might abuse a general grant of power, and since it was prudent to be as specific as could be regarding the extent of its authority, the Convention chose to enumerate the various things which the Congress could do.

But it was otherwise with respect to the limitations upon Congress sought by the men from South Carolina and Georgia. As the debates continued, the Far Southerners proposed that Congress be constitutionally forbidden to levy export taxes, to interfere with the oceanic slave trade, and to pass navigation acts. Their demands were listened to with some sympathy, and a report from the Committee on Detail on August 7 gave them substantially what they wanted. Rutledge was the chairman of the committee. Also upon it were Edmund Randolph, James Wilson, Nathaniel Gorham of Massachusetts, and Oliver Ellsworth of Connecticut. It may well be that even Gorham was then disposed to placate the Far Southerners, for he had written to a relative on July 31: "Great wisdom and prudence, as well as liberality of sentiment and a readiness to surrender natural rights and privileges for the good of the nation appears in the Southern delegates in general," and that he wished "the same spirit may pervade the whole country." It is quite certain that Ellsworth had determined to please the men from the Far South, for he later firmly stood for the limitations they desired. The committee report called for prohibitions with respect to export taxes and the oceanic slave trade, and it provided that navigation acts must have the consent of two-thirds of both houses of Congress, a stipulation which meant that such acts could not be passed without Southern acquiescence, unless the North should grow far greater than the South.

Certainly Wilson did not approve of the committee report, and he and other Northerners fought against its adoption. Wilson was especially opposed to the prohibition of export taxes. He was supported by Washington and Madison, who were willing to run the risk of discriminatory taxes upon the raw materials sent across the ocean by the Southern planters and farmers. But Ellsworth and

Roger Sherman of Connecticut and Elbridge Gerry of Massachusetts spoke for the prohibition, and it was approved. The other limiting clause did not fare so well. Delegates from the Upper South, including George Mason and Luther Martin, were bitter enemies of the Atlantic slave trade. Mason assailed it as an "infernal" traffic which increased the number of slaves, discouraged the immigration of whites into the South, and injured there both the arts and manufacturing. The Carolinians insisted upon the prohibition. Rutledge declared that "religion and humanity had nothing to do with the question." C. C. Pinckney said South Carolina might "by degrees do of herself what is wished," but was positively opposed to federal action. Abraham Baldwin asserted that Georgia also might act against the trade if its regulation were left to the states. C. C. Pinckney and Baldwin were doubtless quite sincere, for the Far South then desired only a temporary addition to the slave labor supply to clear new lands. The Far South had not struggled against a ban upon the trade during wartime imposed by the Congress in 1776. And both the Carolinas and Georgia did move against it between 1787 and 1807. But Mason and Northerners continued to demand that Congress be permitted to act. The two-thirds requirement for navigation laws also aroused keen opposition. It was only too apparent that it might prevent the passage of laws to limit British shipping in American ports—and Northern shipowners wanted to carry the imports and exports of the South. It became clear that the South must make concessions, and the three prohibitions were accordingly referred to a special committee containing one man from each state. The person upon it of the greatest importance, as events were to prove, was C. C. Pinckney.

The select committee brought a compromise back to the Convention, and it was approved, save for one detail, on August 29. In the report, the prohibition against taxation of exports was retained, but Congress was authorized to impose a tax not exceeding ten dollars upon every slave imported and also to regulate the slave trade after 1800. Moreover, navigation acts were to be permitted by simple majorities in both houses of Congress. On the floor, C. C. Pinckney urged that authority to regulate the slave traffic be withheld for twenty years after the adoption of the Constitution, and his request was granted, in view of the generous attitude he and others in the South Carolina delegation displayed toward the welfare of

Northern maritime carriers. Many Southerners, including Charles Pinckney, were reluctant to concede an opportunity to Northern merchants to monopolize the foreign commerce of the South, but C. C. Pinckney insisted upon making the concession. He said, it is reported,

> it was the true interest of the S. states to have no regulation of commerce; but considering the loss brought on the commerce of the Eastern states by the revolution, their liberal conduct towards the views of South Carolina, and the interest the weak Southn. states had in being united with the strong Eastern states, he thought it proper that no fetters should be imposed on the power of making commercial regulations; and that his constituents though prejudiced against the Eastern states, would be reconciled to this liberality—He had himself, he said, prejudices against the Eastern states before he came here, but would acknowledge that he had found them as liberal and candid as any men whatever.

C. C. Pinckney was supported by Rutledge and Pierce Butler—reluctantly by Butler, who had expressed the view that Northern and Southern interests were as opposite as those "of Russia and Turkey." Thus, despite the opposition of Charles

Pinckney, the South Carolina delegation voted for the compromise; and the action of South Carolina, together with the approval which it gained from Northern delegates, insured its acceptance.

The bargain made by the New Englanders and the South Carolinians—by Oliver Ellsworth and C. C. Pinckney, one may say—settled the last major issue between North and South in the Convention. But it caused heart-burning among men from the Upper South, including George Mason and Luther Martin. In the debates concerning it, Mason passionately denounced simple majorities for the regulation of commerce: "The *majority* will be governed by their interests. The Southern states are in the *minority* in both houses [of Congress]. Is it to be expected that they will deliver themselves bound, hand and foot, to the Eastern states and enable them to exclaim, in the words of Cromwell, on a certain occasion—'the Lord hath delivered them into our hands?'" Mason was also unhappy because the compromise permitted the continuance of the oceanic slave trade, which he thoroughly detested, until 1808. Accordingly, on September 13 he urged that two-thirds majorities be made necessary for navigation laws until that year—why should not congressional authority be limited precisely with respect to such laws as it was with regard to the slave traffic? But his proposal received the support only of Virginia, Maryland, and Georgia; North Carolina did not vote; and South Carolina cast her weight against it. Mason then announced that he would fight against the adoption of the Constitution, that there must be a second Convention to alter it.

So it was that North and South reconciled their differences in the Convention, and that body was able to complete the Constitution and present it to the public in September, 1787. Toward securing its adoption, the Convention declared it was to go into effect when ratified by nine state conventions specially chosen to consider it. It would not be easy to secure even such minimum approval. Certainly, many throughout the United States would bitterly struggle against the creation of a strong central government; the omission of a bill of rights, partly because of lack of interest in one, partly because it was thought unnecessary, was to cause alarm among liberal-minded men; and dissatisfaction with specific provisions would make more enemies. Since the Constitution forbade the states to issue paper money and to "impair the obligations of a contract," the champions of paper money and

debtors must be offended. The opposition in the
South would have another ground for complaint:
that Southern interests, despite the concessions
won by the Southern delegates, were not sufficiently protected against arbitrary action on the
part of the North. That the struggle for ratification would be strenuous was indicated by the fact
that Luther Martin and John Francis Mercer
joined Mason in announcing dislike of the product
of the Convention. Moreover, Edmund Randolph
declared that the Constitution must be amended
before being put into effect.

(4)

The South Ratifies
the Constitution

It is a little strange, but the textbooks in general American history and political science used in American colleges and universities do not say that ratification of the Constitution was opposed in the South on sectional as well as other grounds. This even though the historians of Virginia have pointed out time and again that fears for Southern interests played a most important role in the convention of 1788 of that state. Perhaps the narrators of the nation's history, being often Northerners, are not acquainted with the chronicles of the Old Dominion. Perhaps they are not so familiar even with their Jefferson as they would have us believe, for Jefferson declared that the struggle over ratification was sharper in the South than elsewhere—because of the fact that many Southerners believed the Constitution did not offer sufficient protection against Northern domination. Perhaps they have relied too much upon the *Federalist Papers,* which refer only very briefly, although pointedly, to Southern sectionalism, saying that failure to put the Constitution into effect would probably lead to the formation of a Southern confederacy. In small part they may have been deprived of information because the Southern Antifederalists did not trumpet their regional alarms outside the South. George Mason, sending to Northern Antifederalists arguments against the Constitution, carefully omitted his Southern dissatisfactions, which would hardly have given strength to the enemies of the Constitution above the Mason-Dixon line. In Virginia he was ardent, and in Virginia the great decision regarding the Constitution was made. The issue was long doubtful in the Old Dominion; and had Virginia said nay, North Carolina would have persisted in her negative vote. It is hardly necessary to say that an American union without the two states could hardly have been formed, could hardly have endured.

In view of what has been said, particularly concerning the compromise of August 29 in the Convention between New England and South Carolina, it should not surprise that it was easier to secure endorsement of the Constitution in the Far South than it was in the Upper South. We know nothing about ratification by Georgia except that the convention of that state unanimously and quickly gave its approval early in 1788. There are two contemporary statements, not emanating from men on the spot, to the effect that Georgia was threatened by war with the Creek Indians and that the state acted promptly because it wanted the military protection which a strong central government could afford. This explanation doubtless has some merit, for Georgia was still a frontier state. But it cannot be a complete one, especially since a war with the Creeks was then actually desired by some Georgians. It may well be that the compromise of August 29 won support for the Constitution, especially in the long-settled areas. It should be added that the unanimous action of the Convention is not proof that there was no feeling in the state against the Constitution.

If we know little of the course of debate over the Constitution in Georgia, we are much better informed regarding the contest in South Carolina. It began in January, 1788, in the state legislature, when that body considered whether or not to call a convention to consider the Constitution. There was no opposition against the election of the convention, but Rawlins Lowndes, once a political power in South Carolina, with small support from a few other members, opened an attack upon the Constitution. Lowndes declared he was satisfied with the Articles of Confederation, assailed the Constitution because it opened a path to monarchy and gave insufficient defense to Southern interests. He called for a second constitutional convention. He declaimed against congressional power to regulate commerce and to put an end to the oceanic slave trade. Lowndes was unhappy also because the Constitution forbade the states to issue paper money. He voiced fears that the Northerners would secure majorities in Congress, that they would also win the presidency after Washington was no longer available, and that they would use their power to injure South Carolina. The election of a South Carolinian or Georgian to the presidency he considered most unlikely. He declared that "when this new Constitution should be adopted, the sun of the Southern states would set, never to rise again." He also proclaimed that he desired as his epitaph, "Here lies the man that opposed the Constitution because it was ruinous to the liberty of America."

But Lowndes was unable to bear up against the

Pinckneys and Rutledge, who ably defended the document they had helped to make. They said the concessions they had been forced to make to the North were not major. If the North gained control of Southern maritime traffic through navigation acts, which the South might prevent either in Congress or by building her own ships, it was not bad that the North should prosper. The welfare of the South was linked with that of the North. They received potent assistance from Robert Barnwell, who matched Lowndes in appeal to emotion. Barnwell ridiculed efforts to stimulate jealousy of the "Eastern states," reminding his listeners that Northerners had fought to defend South Carolina in the War of Independence and that Lowndes had failed to sacrifice all in the common cause.

When the arm of oppression lay heavy on us, were they not the first to arouse themselves? When the sword of civil discord was drawn, were they not the first in the field? When war deluged their plains with blood, what was their language? Did they demand the southern troops to the defence of the north? No! Or, when war floated to the South, did they withhold their assistance? The answer was the same. When we stood with the spirit, but weakness, of youth, they supported us with

the vigor and precedence of age. When our country was subdued, when our citizens submitted to
superior power, it was then these states evinced
their attachment. He saw not a man who did not
know that the shackles of the south were broken
asunder by the arms of the north.

The assembly had not forgotten the Continentals
and militia who had come southward to fight
against Lord Cornwallis and the British; nor was
it unaware that Lowndes, speaker of the lower
house and champion of American rights before
the war, and also a President of the Revolutionary
Convention of the State, was one of those Carolinians who had "submitted to superior power," for
he had abandoned the struggle as hopeless and had
taken an oath of allegiance to George III. Lowndes
was borne down. He found some allies among members from upcountry (which was likely to oppose
any measure favored by the Low Country), but
he and they could not stand against the Low Country aristocracy.

Ably led by the Pinckneys and the Rutledges,
that aristocracy was heavily over-represented both
in the assembly and in the state convention, which
met at Charleston in the following May. Conceiv-
ably, a plebescite, although it is doubtful, would

have given the victory to the Antifederalists, for they were numerous in the interior of the state, where South Carolina's white population was heaviest. As it was, the champions of the Constitution had great advantages in the contest. Moreover, they did not succumb to overconfidence. Antifederalists sent large quantities of their "literature," including papers by George Mason, to South Carolina, especially to the Piedmont, but the Constitution men put forth their own propaganda. Among them was Dr. David Ramsay, who offered an answer of sorts to almost every sectional objection in "An Address to the Freemen of South Carolina." Especially interesting was his argument against the danger of Northern tyranny. By including Delaware in the South, he created a standoff between "the Northern states" and "the Southern states," with Pennsylvania holding the balance, in the first Congress-to-be. He fancied Pennsylvania would not necessarily vote against the South. In the future the Southern states would be in a position easily to defend themselves in Congress. New England had poor soil, and the numbers of the Yankees would not increase so rapidly as they would in the South. "In fifty years, it is probable," said Ramsay, "that the Southern states will have a great ascendency over the Eastern." Another propagandist for the Constitution was Charles Pinckney who as "A Steady Open Republican" campaigned for it in the *State Gazette of South Carolina.* So well made was the Constitution, with its checks and balances, said he, anticipating orators of a later time, that the hand of God must have guided its makers. It certainly offered a far better system of government than he had hoped for when he went to Philadelphia. He stressed the need of a strong central government for defense, South Carolina and Georgia being weak and menaced by British intrigues and Indian attacks. He claimed Britain would be much pleased if the Lower South were to reject the Constitution: "The three Southern states particularly, we have had for several years past, good grounds to think Great Britain wishes to separate from the rest, and to have reverted to her if possible."

In the elections for members of the Convention, the Federalists won rather easily, carrying the Low Country. Lowndes did not seek a seat in it. The Upcountry generally sent enemies of the Constitution to the convention, but they were definitely in the minority. Their leading spokesmen were General Thomas Sumter, Judge Aedanus Burke, and Dr. Peter Fayssoux; but Mr. P. Dollard of

Prince Frederick Parish probably offered the best summary of their case against the Constitution. Mr. Dollard said his constituents disliked it because it contained no bill of rights, because it opened the way for a tyrannical central government, and because "it was big with political mischiefs and pregnant with a greater variety of impending woes to the good people of the southern states, especially South-Carolina, than all the plagues supposed to issue from the poisonous box of Pandora." Here were the standard arguments of the Southern Antifederalists against the document on the bases of personal, state, and Southern rights. A point-by-point analysis of the Constitution apparently changed few, if any, minds. On May 21 a decisive vote was taken on a motion by Sumter to adjourn until October. It was defeated by a majority of 135 to 89. The final verdict, on May 23, was aye by a vote of 149 to 70.

One concession, a meaningful one, was readily made to the foes of adoption. It was agreed that the South Carolina members in the Congress-to-be should support amendments to the Constitution, including a proviso that the states retained "every power not expressly relinquished by them." Beaten but conciliated, many of the Antifederalists indicated they would graciously accept the outcome. Afterward, both C. C. Pinckney and Edward Rutledge claimed that victory had been easily won for the Constitution, and Pinckney asserted that the Antifederalists had fought against it chiefly because of its clauses protecting rights under contracts and preventing state paper money. But it is apparent that it was not merely champions of debtors who fought against the Constitution, despite Pinckney's claim—we have here a statement by an honest and conservative-minded lawyer. It is equally clear that both Pinckney and Rutledge made too little of the Antifederalist forces in South Carolina. Had the enemies of the Constitution been led by such a one as William Henry Drayton, had the Upcountry not been under-represented, there must have been a more strenuous contest, although the result would possibly have been the same.

Meanwhile, the debate over the Constitution had begun in the Upper South, had indeed begun and ended in Maryland. It had clamorous and vociferous foes east of the Potomac, led by Luther Martin, John Francis Mercer, and Samuel Chase. But these men were not very effective. All of them were in the position of debtors, who might lose financially as a result of adoption, and they were supported by Marylanders who wanted no ban against paper money. While they declaimed about the dangers of creating a central tyranny, they did not vigorously assert Southern sectionalism; and their appeals to the voters lacked authority and passion. Moreover, Washington quietly urged his friends across the Potomac to do all they could for the Constitution, insisting upon speedy ratification. When the ballots for seats in the state convention were counted, it was discovered that the Federalists had a five-to-one majority. Their foes did not abandon the struggle, but continued it vainly in the convention which met at Annapolis late in April, 1788. There they sought to insert amendments, only one of which was peculiarly Southern. It provided that "no regulation of commerce, or navigation act, shall be made, unless with the consent of two thirds of the members of each branch of Congress." It may be significant that this proposal lost by the rather narrow margin of 8 to 5 in a special committee chosen to consider alterations—the Federalists might not have been so solidly in control of the convention had the Antifederalists campaigned more vigorously in defense of Southern interests. But the friends of the Constitution were easily in the saddle. They defeated all attempts to amend it, and they refused even to debate. Their answer to its critics on the floor was a complete silence. Nor would they postpone a final vote until a later time. The Antifederalists in Virginia seemed to be making headway. And those of Maryland believed that, given delay, sentiment would shift in Maryland, especially if Virginia, as seemed quite possible, would not accept less than a prompt and unqualified endorsement, and they pushed it through by the overwhelming majority of 63 to 11.

But if the Federalists won an easy victory in Maryland, they encountered the most bitter opposition in Virginia. The question whether or not the Constitution was to be sanctioned was settled there. When the Virginia convention met in June, 1788, at Richmond, eight states had ratified the document and it was under consideration in New Hampshire. Accordingly, a favorable vote by Virginia would mean that nine or ten states had ratified, and that the Constitution could be put into force. Moreover, North Carolina could hardly persist in the negative after her sister state had given her sanction. On the other hand, if Virginia failed to give her approval, it was quite certain that North Carolina would follow the lead of the Old Dominion, for the Tarheel Antifederalists were even stonger in proportion than those of Virginia.

The Virginia delegates returning from Philadelphia had hardly reached their firesides when a long campaign began against the Constitution. In letters, pamphlets, and speeches there poured forth almost every conceivable argument against it. It contained no bill of rights, and its adoption would lead to the destruction of personal liberties; it would bring back monarchy; it would create a ruling aristocracy; and it protected the abominable slave trade. But above all, the Constitution was a dagger aimed at the South, and its point must be blunted or avoided. It must be amended to protect against all these evils. Were it not possible to secure changes, Virginia must think of creating a Southern federation in which rights of the person, republicanism, and Southern interests would be effectively defended.

The clamor in the Old Dominion against the Constitution was not confined to one class nor to one area in the state. It rose everywhere within its boundaries, and great figures in public life participated in it. One of the more moderate enemies of the Constitution was Richard Henry Lee, long a power at Williamsburg and Richmond, who in his

Letters of a Federal Farmer supplied arguments to Antifederalists everywhere. Although Lee directed his writings to all America, he did not fail to say that the Constitution threatened Southern interests; and he emphatically declared that Congressional authority to regulate commerce was a menace to the South. A two-thirds or even three-fourths majority in both houses should be required for commercial legislation. Said he: "In this congressional legislature a bare majority can enact commercial laws, so that the representatives of seven northern states, as they will have a majority, can, by law, create the most oppressive monopolies upon the five Southern states, whose circumstances and productions are essentially different from theirs, although not a single man of their voters are the representatives of, or amenable to, the people of the southern states. . . . It is supposed that the policy of the southern states will prevent such abuses! but how feeble, sir, is *policy* when opposed to interest among trading people." Far more forthright in denunciation was Benjamin Harrison, who wrote to Washington: "If the constitution is carried into effect, the states south of the potowmac, will be little more than appendages to those to the northward of it . . . in the nature of things they must sooner or later, establish a tyranny, not inferior to the triumvirate or centum viri of Rome."

Equally vigorous language was used by George Mason, who spoke forth both as a champion of liberty and of the South. He wanted amendments protecting both personal and states' rights. He feared the Constitution would bring either oligarchy or monarchy and Northern domination. In it should have been placed arrangements for a council to advise the President consisting of two men from each of the three sections, New England, the Middle states, and the South. That it permitted the passage of commercial laws by a mere majority in Congress was "an insuperable objection," for "the five southern states (whose produce and circumstances are totally different from those of the eight northern and eastern states) will be ruined."

Especially ominous for the cause of the Constitution was the hostility of Patrick Henry. Still the orator incomparable, the Henry of the winter of 1787–1788 and the spring following was not that Henry who had so ardently proclaimed himself above all an American in St. John's church in 1775. The great pleader was now no stout nationalist. He was, indeed, to a degree a political weathervane, shifting with public opinion and sentiment. Able still to sway an audience, especially an unsophisticated one, he might be distrusted, as he was by Jefferson; he was no feeble antagonist in argument or politics. He gathered about him all the enemies of the Constitution, including those who would accept it with substantial changes and those who wanted none of it. He said he desired the Constitution much and suitably altered. He astutely appealed to the reasoning powers and especially to the emotions of his fellow Virginians. He was fighting in behalf of the plain planter against aristocrats who would use the Constitution to create a detestable oligarchy. He aroused the fears of men indebted to British merchants: those grasping enemy creditors would make use of the Federal courts-to-be. He pointed out to paper money advocates that their cause would be destroyed by the Constitution. To the Kentuckians and other Virginians long since angry because Congress had failed to secure the opening of the Mississippi, Henry said that a central government dominated by Northerners would neglect to secure the right of navigation. Moreover, the Northerners would control that government, and they would discriminate grievously against the Southern people whenever they could so secure gain for themselves.

Washington was shocked and alarmed by the arguments and the vehemence of Henry, Mason, and their cohorts. "It is a little strange," he wrote to Lafayette, "that the men of large property in the South, should be more afraid that the Constitution will produce an aristocracy or a monarchy, than the genuine democratical people of the East." To fellow Virginian David Stuart he defended legislation over navigation by simple majority. "I am mistaken if any three men, bodies of men, or countries, will enter into any compact or treaty if *one* of the three is to have a negative controul over the other two. There must be a reciprocity or no union, which is preferable will not become a question in the mind of any true patriot. But granting it to be an evil, it will infallibly work its own cure, and an ultimate advantage to the Southern states." To Stuart he also expressed suspicion—one that was shared by other Virginia Federalists—that Mason, Henry, and their most ardent followers sought to create a Southern federation. He said, "That there are some writers (and others perhaps who may not have written) who wish to see these states divided into several confederacies is pretty evident." Unable to seek election to the state convention, since he would thus expose himself to a charge that he was pushing for the presidency, Washington quietly encouraged the Virginia Federalists to do battle. They were not reluctant to engage and formed behind Madison. They won an important victory when they managed to persuade Edmund Randolph, then governor, to stand for the Constitution and to seek the amendments he desired at a later time rather than to insist upon them prior to adoption—a victory which provoked Mason into describing Randolph as a young Benedict Arnold.

When the convention met, the friends of the Constitution on the one hand and its foes and doubters on the other seemed almost equally divided. The region south of the James River, and Kentucky had sent many men who did not admire the document; northern Virginia in general elected men who favored it. Probably the Federalists had a small majority among the 168 members, although Henry claimed otherwise until the end of its sessions, which consumed three weeks. Certainly the Federalists had an advantage in leadership. Henry and Mason, backed by James Monroe and William Grayson, were formidable enough. They were without the aid of Richard Henry Lee, however, for he had excused himself from seeking election on the score of illness. Although the great leader of the forces for the Constitution could not be present, his pervasive influence was felt from Mount Vernon. On the spot were Madison, the veteran and respected politician Edmund Pendleton, and the influential Randolph. Supporting them were George Nicholas, George Innes, and the Continental veterans and devoted nationalists, Light-Horse Harry Lee and John Marshall.

There were long debates over the document, which was examined bit by bit at the request of Henry, who seems to have believed that it was good tactics to assail almost every detail of the Constitution. With Henry taking the principal role, the Antifederalists did indeed find almost every conceivable fault. The arguments offered by Mason and Henry earlier in behalf of Southern interests, republicanism, and personal rights, were again and again brought forth. Henry even charged that treaties, despite the two-thirds majority required for them in the Senate, would be made without the consent of the South and against her well-being. He claimed that members of Congress could arrogantly vote themselves large salaries, that the Federal district would become an asylum for escaped slaves. He asserted that Congress might free all the slaves during some future war upon the excuse of prosecuting it more effectively. He saw national authority over the militia as dangerous to freedom. In the heat of the contest he went so far as to say that the Constitution was inferior to that of monarchist Britain.

The arguments offered by Henry and his allies were not without validity, as events were to prove. But he and they made too much of small matters, and Henry found faults which did not exist. Had he continuously pounded at major issues, avoiding ill-founded criticism, had he devoted his oratory to generals rather than to particulars, he might have been more effective. As it was, his behavior was akin to that of a pettifogging lawyer; and while his tactics might have succeeded with plain farmers on a jury, they probably had little influence upon the more sophisticated men who sat in the convention. Madison, upon whom chiefly fell the burden of answering Henry, was not an eloquent man. Moreover, he was suffering from "a bilious attack," and he was so feeble that at times he could not be heard. But his quiet answers to Henry's charges were well put and as convincing as might be. Point by point, he destroyed or weakened Henry's objections. He dammed Henry with faint phrase. The Constitution was not perfect, but as good as might have been made. Toward making it, both Northerners and Southerners had sacrificed. A strong central government would surely deal more effectively with the Mississippi question than a weak one. Other Southern concerns were sufficiently cared for; and if by any chance they were not, time and the rapid growth of Southern population would certainly put an end to Northern abuses of power in Congress. The new central government would provide effectively for defense; yet its authority was limited enough so that personal liberties and states' rights were safe. If there were faults, they could be corrected later by amendment. There must be no attempt to amend the Constitution before it was adopted. Such an attempt would doubtless prevent adoption.

Madison was firmly supported by a well-organized corps of debaters who were more effective than Henry's principal followers. Randolph, Pendleton, Nicholas, and Marshall lent strength to Madison. But the most persuasive of them was Light-Horse Harry Lee. His friends were polite to Henry, even when the orator was plainly engaged in obfuscation. Lee, who had offered brilliant service throughout the war, was a sharp-tongued cavalryman. He would not let Henry pose as the great and exclusive champion of "liberty," a word that frequently came from Henry's lips. Lee had fought for liberty, and he would put his record in her behalf beside that of Henry. He expressed contempt for Henry's "windings and turnings." Lee even harshly expressed a low opinion of the orator's intellect. "The honorable gentleman is so little used to triumph on the grounds of reasoning, that he suffers himself to be captivated by the least appearance of victory." Here was rude and personal attack which may not have won sympathy, but which put the Federalists on the offensive. And having descended to personalities, Lee then announced his allegiance to the nation and to the Constitution in language which Washington might have used, had he been present. Indeed, Lee's listeners must have heard in his phrases the voice of Mount Vernon.

In the course of Saturday, and some previous harangues, from the terms in which some of the Northern states were spoken of, one would have thought that the love of an American was in some degree criminal, as being incompatible with a proper degree of affection for a Virginian. The people of America, sir, are one people. I love the people of the north, not because they have adopted the Constitution, but because I fought

with them as my countrymen, and because I consider them as such. Does it follow from hence that
I have forgotten my attachment to my native
state? In all local matters I shall be a Virginian:
in those of a general nature, I shall not forget that
I am an American.

Henry and his cohorts were defeated in argument, but it was not certain until the very end of
the convention that the Federalists had a majority.
It has often been suggested that they would have
encountered defeat had not Randolph as governor
temporarily kept quiet the contents of a letter
from Governor George Clinton of New York which
declared that that state would ratify only with
many clogging amendments. It is at least equally
likely, probably more so, that men's minds were
quite made up at the beginning of the convention,
that the Federalists had a majority then, that they
maintained it during the course of the debates,
and that the behavior of New York would not have
affected the outcome. On June 25 prior amendments were voted down 88 to 80, and the Constitution was definitely sanctioned on the same day,
89 to 79. There can be no doubt that it was Washington who was ultimately responsible for the triumph of the Constitution-men. "Be assured," wrote

Monroe to Jefferson soon after the verdict was reached, "that his influence carried this government." It was not merely that Washington exerted himself in behalf of the Constitution. As James McHenry later wrote to the general—after he had become President—the expectation that Washington would be chosen, "I am sure had a secret and powerful influence in disposing the minds of the people to embrace the new Constitution."

How truly massive were the fears in Virginia of central and Northern tyranny appeared at the very close of the state convention. Sanctioning the Constitution, the convention also insisted that the rights of the states must be respected and that the right of revolution remained. Further, it unanimously called for a bill of personal rights. In addition, a few of the Federalists joined with Henry's following to create a majority which demanded other amendments to protect Southern interests. These would have required ratification of "commercial" treaties by two-thirds of the membership of the Senate rather than of those senators present; approval of treaties ceding territory or rights of navigation both by two-thirds of the Senate and three-fourths of the states; and the familiar two-thirds majority for laws governing navigation and commerce. Nor did those who demanded changes abandon their efforts after the convention had dissolved. Elected governor, Henry drove hard for amendments. Not until Madison had begun to push through Congress the Federal bill of rights did the cry for changes diminish in Virginia.

Even so, Virginia had taken the decisive step; and since New Hampshire had already voted favorably, ten states had given their sanction to the Constitution. New York then climbed on the bandwagon, and only North Carolina and Rhode Island were still outside the union obviously to be formed. Both were constrained to act affirmatively, and both finally did.

Had Virginia insisted upon revision of the Constitution, North Carolina, again, would almost certainly have taken the same stand. In the Tarheel country there was no powerful and well-led Tidewater aristocracy like that of South Carolina. Aristocrats were relatively fewer in North Carolina, even in the coastal counties, and the Piedmont was not so grossly under-represented as it was south of the Peedee River. Moreover, the Piedmont was disposed to oppose any measure favored by Tidewater. Accordingly, the yeoman farmers of the state ultimately had the decision in their hands. They found the views of George Mason and Patrick Henry, which were widely circulated, much to their liking. They were eager to defend liberty, republicanism, and Southern interests. The Federalists, including Hugh Williamson and James Iredell, answered the arguments of Mason and Henry in newspaper letters and pamphlets, but to no avail. Both the Federalists and their opponents used strong language regarding each other, and even the almost sacred Washington was abused. Thomas Person, a violent antagonist of the Constitution, described Washington as "a damned rascal and traitor to his country for putting his name to such an infamous paper as the new Constitution." When the state legislature was asked, in December, 1787, to issue a call for the election of a convention, Antifederalists led by Person not only denounced the Constitution, but spoke against holding a convention. However, it seemed just to fair-minded men in that body to put the great question to a trial. Arrangements were made for the election, which took place in March, 1788, the convention convening at Hillsboro on July 21.

In that convention the friends of the Constitution were in a decided minority. Two of their leaders, Richard Caswell and William Hooper, had been defeated at the polls; and they had carried only the Tidewater country. The Antifederalists had a majority of more than two to one. There was some debate, the issues discussed being substantially the same as in the Virginia convention, the arguments being also similar. But the canvass was brief, for the opponents of the Constitution, following the leadership of Willie Jones, would not waste much time in answering James Iredell and other Federalist champions. They had the votes, 184 to 84, and they wanted to use them quickly. On August 2 they put through their program, calling for a second Federal convention and a revised Constitution containing chiefly the amendments proposed by George Mason and Patrick Henry. Wrote Iredell to his wife, "We are . . . for the present out of the union and God knows when we shall get into it again."

Actually, since Virginia had already acceded, North Carolina was out of the union, but could not stay out. A Southern confederacy had become impossible, and a permanently independent republic of North Carolina was equally impossible. In September, 1788, Person and Jones are reported as saying that North Carolina should refrain from ratifying the Constitution for five or six years, should wait and see whether the new system was as vicious as they had said it would be. But a North Carolinian who called himself "A Republican," in an essay published in the New York *Daily Advertiser* that same month, correctly analyzed sentiment in his state and indicated how to overcome Person and Jones. The North Carolina Antifederalists, said "A Republican," were not seriously against the Constitution because its provisions might force them to pay their debts, and in hard money. They were much more alarmed because of the menaces to Southern interests which they found in it. But they would very reluctantly, if necessary, abandon their efforts to secure more constitutional safeguards for the South, provided that they were given a Federal bill of rights.

Before the end of 1788 sober second thought in North Carolina persuaded the legislature that the Constitution must be reconsidered, and a call for a second convention, which met in the fall of 1789, was issued. Before its election the awkwardness of North Carolina's position with reference to the union had become evident. Although the new Federal Congress carefully avoided treating North Carolina as a foreign country, it was not certain that it would continue to do so indefinitely. Moreover, champions of Southern interests in both the

Carolinas began to urge ratification so as to strengthen the Southern vote at New York. And Madison announced in May, 1789, that he would introduce in Congress amendments providing for a bill of rights. The result was a great shift of opinion. The second North Carolina convention was as overwhelmingly Federalist as the first one had been massively Antifederalist. There was little contention in it, and the Constitution was endorsed by a vote of 193 to 75.

The South had entered the union without securing all the constitutional safeguards against domination by the central government which so many of her people so ardently desired.

(5)

Aftermath

In April, 1789, announcing the unanimous election of Washington to the presidency, a writer in a Maryland newspaper declared that "this very singular event displays to the astonished world, an empire of dissimiliar climes, products, and interests, listening to the simple and enlightened voice of reason." But if all the American people listened to the "voice of reason" in electing Washington, there was no oracle then or afterward, which persuaded North and South that they had naught that was basic about which to quarrel; and Southern sectionalism was to endure, reaching a climax in 1861. It was to wax and wane, increasing when the central government was under the sway of hostile Northerners, lessening when Southerners and Northerners friendly to the South dominated in the national capital.

Surely that Southern sectionalism which made

its appearance with the nation did not disappear below the Mason-Dixon line in 1789, to revive only when the Old South began to emerge about 1820. In January of the year of Washington's inauguration, a Virginian declared that "the Southern States" should avoid electing young bachelors to Congress. They might marry Northern belles and fail to defend Southern interests. He wished the national capital to be at Williamsburg. "To the North they never seem to have had an eye to New-Virginia, Kentucky, the Carolinas, and Georgia; but it must be hinted to them, or we shall shortly, very shortly perhaps, have another Congress at Richmond." During Washington's first term, law after law was enacted by Congress to the special benefit of the North. The prediction of the Southern Antifederalists that the Constitution would become an instrument for Northern tyranny seemed to many Southern Federalists about to come true. As early as September, 1789, William Grayson, then a United States senator, wrote gloatingly but gloomily to Patrick Henry that the Virginia Federalists would

e'er long, have abundant cause to conclude, that the idea of a difference between carrying states and productive states and manufacturing states and slave states is not a mere phantom of the imagination. If they reflect at all on the meaning of protective duties . . . I think they would now agree that we were not totally beside ourselves in the [Virginia] convention. In my opinion, whenever the impost bill comes into action, the friends of the South will be let into some secrets that they do not or will not at present apprehend. You would be astonished at the progress of manufacturers in the seven easternmost states, if they go on in the same proportion for seven years, they will pay very little on imports, while the South will continue to labor under the pressure.

By 1791, indeed, Southerners who had favored the Constitution were joining Southerners who had opposed it to defend Southern interests and to form the Democratic-Republican faction for that purpose. So high ran sectional feeling in the South by 1792 that in May of that year Jefferson urged Washington to run for re-election in order to soften Southern feeling. "The confidence of the whole union is centered in you. Your being at the helm will be more than an answer to every argument which can be used to alarm and lead the people in any quarter, into violence and secession.

North and South will hang together if they have you to hang on." The re-election of Washington, said Jefferson, would give time; and he hoped that census returns would later so strengthen the South at the national capital that the North would be unable to push through measures so desperately disliked in the South.

Washington was also alarmed in that month of May. He was well aware that Northern men led by Alexander Hamilton had thus far had their way at the national capital. The remedy, as he saw it, was not disunion, but effective political opposition by the Southerners. Beginning to prepare his Farewell Address, he informed Madison that he wanted to tell the American people that "we are *all* the children of the same country; a country great and rich in itself; capable, and promising to be, as prosperous and happy as any the annals of history have ever brought to our view. That our interest, however, deversified in local and smaller matters, is the same in all the great and essential concerns of the nation." The problem of South versus North continued to worry Washington. In the Farewell Address as it was given to the public in 1796, the themes he had mentioned to Madison were discussed in detail, for he devoted much more space to domes-

tic difficulties in that solemn testament than to en-
tangling alliances, more even than to foreign affairs as a whole. Extolling the union, he adjured
his countrymen to concentrate their affections upon
the nation and to take pride above all in the name
AMERICAN. They had fought and triumphed together in the cause of independence and liberty.
But it was even more important for them to recognize, he said, the fundamental identity of interests
among them. Both North and South were prosper-
ing; the differences between them, and those between East and West, must not be exaggerated.
Condemning political parties, he denounced especially parties based on sectional divergences; their
leaders made too much of such differences for their
own purposes and deceived their followers.

So long as Washington was active in the political arena, he was able to soften sectional strife. His
advice in the Farewell Address could not sway the
minds of men afterward. In 1798 came the vehe-
ment denunciation of national tyranny in the
Kentucky Resolutions, which virtually put forth
the doctrine of nullification. The election to the
presidency of Jefferson at the beginning of the new
century and the long-continued ascendancy of the
Democratic-Republicans under Jefferson, Madison,

and Monroe, soothed the South. However, as Jefferson walked to his inauguration, slavery was virtually dead in the North; and the census of 1800 revealed that the North was growing more rapidly in numbers than the South. The South was to fall more and more decidedly into a minority position; the Northern attack upon slavery would come. In the time of the Old South, the position which Washington took in the era of the First South did not have its pristine appeal.

Bibliographical Note

These Fleming Lectures are not based upon a quantity of newly discovered and hitherto unused materials. Rather they are principally founded upon published records, correspondence, and diaries, together with newspaper letters and essays, of the Revolutionary period. If the author has made a contribution of importance to learning, it lies in the formulation of a new concept derived from examination of documents mostly available in print. Since the lectures attempt to establish that Southern sectionalism appeared with the American republic, much of their content, consisting of descriptions and analyses of political struggles between the the South and the remainder of the nation, has necessarily been drawn from the records of legislatures and constitutional conventions and the papers of men who played important roles in public life. The author has elsewhere recently published a selective bibliography concerning the South during the era of independence,[1] to which

[1] *The South in the Revolution, 1763–1789* (*A History of the South,* ed. Wendell H. Stephenson and E. Merton Coulter, III [Baton Rouge, 1957]), 401–26.

the reader may be referred for a fuller list of the major sources consulted in the preparation of these lectures. It seems desirable, however, to indicate here the materials of which greatest use has been made.

Primary materials of the greatest value for the study of sectionalism as manifested in official bodies are to be found in Worthington C. Ford *et al.* (eds.) *Journals of the Continental Congress, 1774–1789* (34 vols., Washington, 1904–37); Edmund C. Burnett (ed.), *Letters of Members of the Continental Congress, 1774–1789* (8 vols., Washington, 1921–36); Max Farrand (ed.), *The Records of the Federal Convention of 1787* (4 vols., New Haven, 1911-37); Gaillard Hunt and James B. Scott (eds.), *The Debates in the Federal Convention of 1787* (New York, 1920); *Documentary History of the Constitution of the United States, 1787–1870* (5 vols., Washington, 1894–1905); Jonathan Elliot (ed.), *The Debates in the Several State Conventions on the Adoption of the Federal Constitution* (5 vols., Philadelphia, 1859), a valuable collection that will be replaced in the near future by a new compilation of documents concerning the adoption of the Constitution and the Federal bill of rights in preparation by Robert E. Cushman; Peter Force (comp.), *American Archives,* 4th ser. (6 vols., Washington, 1837–46); 5th ser. (3 vols., Washington, 1848–53); William L. Saunders (ed.), *The Colonial Records of North Carolina* (10 vols., Raleigh, 1886–90); Walter Clark (ed.), *The State Records of North Carolina, 1777–1790* (16 vols., Goldsboro, 1895–1905); *Debates and Other Proceedings of the Convention of Virginia* (Richmond, 1805).

Much light is also thrown upon the rise of the southern "interest," and manifestations of it, in the published papers of men active in public life. Of great value were: Charles Francis Adams (ed.), *The Works of John Adams* (10 vols., Boston, 1850–56); Henry Cabot Lodge (ed.), *The Works of Alexander Hamilton* (11 vols., New York, 1904); William Wirt Henry, *Patrick Henry: Life, Correspondence, and Speeches* (3 vols., New York, 1891); Griffith J. McRee, *Life and Correspondence of James Iredell* (2 vols., New York, 1857–58); Henry P. Johnson (ed.), *The Correspondence and Public Papers of John Jay* (4 vols., New York, 1890–93); Julian P. Boyd *et al.* (eds.), *The Papers of Thomas Jefferson* (Princeton, 1950–); *Letters of Joseph Jones of Virginia, 1777–1787* (Washington, 1889); Charles R. King, (ed.), *The Life and Correspondence of Rufus King* (6 vols., New York, 1894–1900); Isaac O. Leake, *Memoir of the Life and Times of General John Lamb* (Albany, 1850); James C. Ballagh (ed.), *The Letters of Richard Henry Lee* (2 vols., New York, 1911–14); Bernard C. Steiner, *The Life and Correspondence of James McHenry* (Cleveland, 1907); Gaillard Hunt (ed.), *The Writings of James Madison* (9 vols., New York, 1900–10); Kate M. Rowland, *The Life of George Mason* (2 vols., New York, 1902); Stanislaus M. Hamilton (ed.), *The Writings of James Monroe* (7 vols., New York, 1898–1903); John C. Fitzpatrick (ed.), *The Writings of George Washington . . . 1745–1799* (39 vols., Washington, 1931–44).

Other publications containing contemporary writings which were very useful include: [James Anderson],

Free Thoughts on the American Contest (Edinburgh, 1776); Jonathan Boucher, *A View of the Causes and Consequences of the American Revolution* (London, 1797); William K. Boyd (ed.), "News, Letters and Documents Concerning North Carolina and the Federal Constitution," *Trinity College Historical Society Papers*, XIV (1922), 75–95; *The Federalist* (various editions); Paul Leicester Ford (ed.), *Pamphlets on the Constitution of the United States, Published during Its Discussion by the People 1787–1788* (Brooklyn, 1888); Paul Leicester Ford (ed.), *Essays on the Constitution of the United States Published during the Discussion by the People 1787–1788* (Brooklyn, 1892); Frank Moore (comp.), *Diary of the American Revolution* (2 vols., New York, 1858); Hezekiah Niles (comp.), *Principles and Acts of the Revolution in America* (New York, 1876); David Ramsay, *History of the American Revolution* (2 vols., Philadelphia, 1789); and Lyon G. Tyler, *The Letters and Times of the Tylers* (2 vols., Richmond, 1884–85).

Most helpful of the newspapers consulted, because a detailed account of the struggle over ratification of the Constitution in South Carolina has not yet been published, were those of Charleston, including the *Morning Post and Daily Advertiser,* and the *State Gazette of South-Carolina.* Also of special help was the *Maryland Journal and Baltimore Advertiser.*

Secondary works of considerable usefulness in the preparation of these lectures were: Irving Brant, *James Madison the Nationalist, 1780–1787* (Indianapolis,

1948); Irving Brant, *James Madison, Father of the Constitution, 1787–1800* (Indianapolis, 1950); Carl Bridenbaugh, *Myths and Realities: Societies of the Colonial South* (Baton Rouge, 1952); Edmund C. Burnett, *The Continental Congress* (New York, 1941); Moncure Conway, *Omitted Chapters of History Disclosed in the Life and Papers of Edmund Randolph* (New York, 1888); Philip A. Crowl, *Maryland during and after the Revolution* (Baltimore, 1943); Philip A. Crowl, "Anti-Federalism in Maryland, 1787–1788," *William and Mary Quarterly*, 3rd ser., IV (1947), 446–69; Max Farrand, "Compromises of the Constitution," in *Annual Report, 1903* (Washington: American Historical Association, 1904), I, 71–84; Hugh B. Grigsby, *The History of the Virginia Federal Convention of 1788*, in *Collections of the Virginia Historical Society* (Richmond), new ser., IX–X (1890–91); Merrill Jensen, *The Articles of Confederation* (Madison, 1940); Merrill Jensen, *The New Nation: A History of the United States during the Confederation, 1781–1789* (New York, 1950); Hugh T. Lefler and Albert R. Newsome, *North Carolina, the History of a Southern State* (Chapel Hill, 1954); Orin J. Libby, *The Geographical Distribution of the Vote of the Thirteen States on the Federal Constitution, 1787–8* (Madison, 1894); David J. Mays, *Edmund Pendleton, 1721–1803* (2 vols., Cambridge, 1952); Albert R. Newsome, "North Carolina's Ratification of the Federal Constitution," *North Carolina Historical Review*, XVII (1940), 287–301; Robert A. Rutland, *The Birth of the Bill of Rights, 1776–1791*

(Chapel Hill, 1955); Jennings B. Sanders, "Thomas Burke in the Continental Congress," *North Carolina Historical Review,* IX (1932), 22–37; William A. Schaper, *Sectionalism and Representation in South Carolina,* in *Annual Report, 1900* (Washington: American Historical Association, 1901), I, 237–463; Edward P. Smith, "The Movement Towards a Second Constitutional Convention in 1788," in *Essays on the Constitutional History of the United States, 1775–1789,* ed. J. Franklin Jameson (Boston, 1889); Louise I. Trenholme, *The Ratification of the Federal Constitution in North Carolina* (New York, 1932); David D. Wallace, *The History of South Carolina* (4 vols., New York, 1934); and Charles Warren, *The Making of the Constitution* (Boston, 1929).

Index